SpringerBriefs in Law

SpringerBriefs present concise summaries of cutting-edge research and practical applications across a wide spectrum of fields. Featuring compact volumes of 50 to 125 pages, the series covers a range of content from professional to academic. Typical topics might include:

- A timely report of state-of-the art analytical techniques
- A bridge between new research results, as published in journal articles, and a contextual literature review
- A snapshot of a hot or emerging topic
- A presentation of core concepts that students must understand in order to make independent contributions

SpringerBriefs in Law showcase emerging theory, empirical research, and practical application in Law from a global author community. SpringerBriefs are characterized by fast, global electronic dissemination, standard publishing contracts, standardized manuscript preparation and formatting guidelines, and expedited production schedules.

Paula Wojcikiewicz Almeida ·
Vitor Furtado de Melo · Lucas Vollers ·
Valentine Tissot Pinheiro

Uncovering Global South Narratives in ITLOS Advisory Proceedings on Climate Change

A Mixed-Method Approach for Articulating Political and Legal Arguments

Springer

Paula Wojcikiewicz Almeida
Director of Jean Monnet Centre of Excellence on EU-LA Global Challenges (CEJM), co-funded by the European Union, and of FGV Centre for Global Law
Getulio Vargas Foundation (FGV)
Rio de Janeiro, Rio de Janeiro, Brazil

Vitor Furtado de Melo
FGV Centre for Global Law
Getulio Vargas Foundation (FGV)
Rio de Janeiro, Rio de Janeiro, Brazil

Lucas Vollers
FGV Centre for Global Law
Getulio Vargas Foundation (FGV)
Rio de Janeiro, Rio de Janeiro, Brazil

Valentine Tissot Pinheiro
LLM in Public International Law
University of Amsterdam
Rio de Janeiro, Rio de Janeiro, Brazil

ISSN 2192-855X ISSN 2192-8568 (electronic)
SpringerBriefs in Law
ISBN 978-3-032-08426-2 ISBN 978-3-032-08427-9 (eBook)
https://doi.org/10.1007/978-3-032-08427-9

This Springer imprint is published by the registered company Springer Nature Switzerland AG.
The registered company address is: Gewerbestrasse 11, 6330 Cham, Switzerland

Acknowledgements The authors would like to extend their gratitude to the researchers of FGV Rio Law's Centre for Global Law and the Jean Monnet Centre of Excellence on EU-LA GLOBAL (2023–2026), co-funded by the European Union, for their valuable help in conducting research and in discussing preliminary versions of this text. All figures and tables featured in the book and the appendix were developed by the authors. Unauthorised reproduction without proper credit is disallowed.

Co-funded by
the European Union

Views and opinions expressed are however those of the author(s) only and do not necessarily reflect those of the European Union or the European Education and Culture Executive Agency (EACEA). Neither the European Union nor EACEA can be held responsible for them.

The authors would like to thank colleagues from the Université Paris 1 Panthéon-Sorbonne, the Max Planck Institute for Comparative Public Law and International Law and the iCourts (Danish National Research Foundation's Centre of Excellence for International Courts and Governance) for their valuable feedback in previous versions of this research.

Competing Interests The authors have no competing interests to declare that are relevant to the content of this manuscript.

About This Book

Climate change has increasingly been understood as a ‘community interest’, reflecting a fundamental value that cannot be left to the free disposition of individual international actors. However, current international politics limit global achievements on climate change. In this context, international courts and tribunals (ICTs) have been provoked to fill in the gaps of climate inaction, notably via their advisory function. Multiple states have participated during the proceedings of the advisory opinion on climate change issued by the International Tribunal for the Law of the Sea (ITLOS), and Global South states were particularly engaged in these proceedings. Considering that states advance narratives before ICTs and that these stories may reflect their broader political strategies on global issues, the present research focuses on perceiving how and with what aim Global South states’ narratives are articulated in the ITLOS advisory proceedings on climate change. The study examines whether states’ narratives at ICTs are articulated with a broader political context, reflecting their interests expressed in other international arenas. Specifically, it analyses if the Global South states’ narratives advanced during the ITLOS advisory proceedings on climate change echo a common history of colonialism, uneven development, and unequal impacts of climate change.

Contents

About the Authors

Paula Wojcikiewicz Almeida Professor of International Law, Getulio Vargas Foundation Law School in Rio de Janeiro (since 2008). Director of the Centre for Global Law at the Getulio Vargas Foundation Law School. Director of the Jean Monnet Centre of Excellence on EU–Latin America Global Challenges, sponsored by the European Commission (2023–2026). Director of the Jean Monnet Centre of Excellence on EU–South America Global Governance (2019–2023). Associate researcher at the Institute of International and European Law at the Sorbonne (IREDIES). Permanent professor of the Post-Graduate Program of the Getulio Vargas Foundation Law School in Rio de Janeiro. Chair of the International Courts and Tribunals Interest Group of the Latin American Society of International Law. Doctorate with honors Summa Cum Laude in International and European Law at the Université Paris 1 Panthéon-Sorbonne. Master's of law in Public International and European Law–Université Paris XI, Faculté Jean Monnet. Researcher at the Centre d'études et de recherche en droit international et relations internationales de l'Académie de droit International de La Haye (2010). Post-doctoral visiting scholar at the Max Planck Institute for Comparative Public Law and International Law (2014; 2025) and at the University of Oxford, Faculty of Law (2014). Visiting professor at the École de Droit de la Sorbonne, Université Paris 1 Panthéon-Sorbonne (2019; 2024). Visiting professor at the European Private Law Summer School at the Faculty of Law of the University of Salzburg (since 2015). Visiting professor at the International Studies Programme of the Master's Degree in International and European law at the Porto School of Law of Universidade Católica (since 2023). Director of studies of the French-Speaking Section in the 6th Edition of the Winter Courses on International Law, organized by the Hague Academy of International Law (2024). ORCID: https://orcid.org/0000-0002-5899-9254.

Valentine Tissot Pinheiro LL.M. in Public International Law (International and European Law) from the University of Amsterdam. LL.B in Law from the Federal University of Rio Grande do Sul (UFRGS). ORCID: https://orcid.org/0009-0000-4841-9183.

Lucas da Cunha Vollers Researcher at FGV Rio Law's Jean Monnet Centre of Excellence on EU-LA Global Challenges, co-funded by the European Commission, and the Centre for Global Law. Master in International Law from the State University of Rio de Janeiro (UERJ). LL.B. in Law from the Pontifical Catholic University of Rio de Janeiro (PUC-Rio). ORCID: https://orcid.org/0009-0004-9460-0935.

Vitor Furtado de Melo Researcher at FGV Rio Law's Jean Monnet Centre of Excellence on EU-LA Global Challenges, co-funded by the European Commission, and the Centre for Global Law. Master in Political Science (UNIRIO), Msc candidate in Social Anthropology (MN/UFRJ), and LL.B. in Law (UNIRIO). ORCID: https://orcid.org/0000-0002-3933-8442.

List of Figures

Chapter 1
Introduction

Abstract This book explores how Global South states construct legal narratives in the advisory proceedings on climate change before the International Tribunal for the Law of the Sea (ITLOS). It frames climate change as a matter of 'community interest' that demands collective action and legal interpretation within international institutions. The study argues that the narratives advanced by Global South states are not merely legal texts but may be embedded within broader political contexts and informed by historical inequalities, colonial legacies, and disproportionate climate vulnerabilities. Drawing on a mixed-method approach, the research examines whether and how these narratives reflect shared demands for climate justice and align with political positions expressed in multilateral arenas, such as the Conferences of the Parties (COPs) of the United Nations Framework Convention on Climate Change (UNFCCC). By analysing Global South states' submissions and discourses, the book sheds light on how legal language operates as a strategic tool of foreign legal policy, shaping and reflecting international legal development through institutionalized adjudication.

Keywords Climate change · Global South · International courts and tribunals · Community interest · Legal narratives

Climate change represents a prominent example of 'community interest', 'collective interest', or 'common concern'.[1] It reflects a fundamental value that cannot be left to the free disposition of individual international actors but is instead a matter of consideration to all states.[2] As an example of community interest, the climate concern reflects a multi-layered value system that is not limited to a formal

[1] Simma (1994).

[2] Ibid, 233.

P. Wojcikiewicz Almeida et al., *Uncovering Global South Narratives in ITLOS Advisory Proceedings on Climate Change*, SpringerBriefs in Law,
https://doi.org/10.1007/978-3-032-08427-9_1

definition and specific normative status, such as *ius cogens* norms, obligations *erga omnes,* or obligations *erga omnes partes*.[3]

Issues concerning climate change are often complex and multifaceted. In the international sphere, mitigation and adaptation actions have been hard to identify,[4] and negotiations in this regard have been slow in comparison with climate change's fast-paced effects.[5] The pursuance of community interests, as those embodied in climate change, depends on the existence of an institutional structure on a global level.[6] As a component of the international governance structure, International Courts and Tribunals (ICTs) can act as organs of the international community entrusted to safeguard its fundamental values, contributing to overcoming collective challenges,[7] such as climate change's consequences.

Particularly, the development of international law applicable to climate change could profit from the ICTs' advisory function that may furnish international actors with stable standards,[8] normative expectations, and authoritative benchmarks.[9] Advisory opinions exercise public judicial function[10] insofar as they create shared normative expectations and influence the behaviour of their addressees.[11] These authoritative interpretations are central to the proper implementation of international law and to supporting compliance with international norms.[12] As far as the climate change regime is concerned, the use of advisory opinions can be utterly relevant to provide clarity over the rules and obligations through the submission of legal questions before an ICT.[13]

Under this context, the International Tribunal on the Law of the Sea (ITLOS), one of the dispute settlement mechanisms envisaged under the United Nations Convention on the Law of the Sea (UNCLOS),[14] is a prominent example of the technical depth and outreach of public interests in international law.[15] Since the UNCLOS provides few human rights obligations,[16] the Tribunal is fully conscious of the embedded community interests of the cases before it and has even noted the

[3] Benzing (2006), 369–371.

[4] Rajamani and Peel (2021), 1039.

[5] Gray et al. (2016), 418.

[6] Simma (1994), 285.

[7] von Bogdandy and Venzke (2013), 49.

[8] Von Bogdandy and Venzke (2011), 1341.

[9] Zimmermann et al. (2019), 36l.

[10] Wiik (2018), 505–506.

[11] Von Bogdandy and Venzke (2011), 979.

[12] Chayes and Chayes (1998), 209–210.

[13] Klein (2021) 1038. at 1052.

[14] For the other means for settling disputes concerning the interpretation or application of UNCLOS, refer to Article 287 (1), United Nations Convention on the Law of the Sea 1982, 1833 UNTS 397.

[15] Tanaka (2011), 329.

[16] Cohen and Afogo (2023).

binding and *erga omnes* character of the obligation to protect and preserve the marine environment.[17] ITLOS may serve to 'consolidate contributions in matters of public interests, as well as the link between the law of the sea and other rules of international law'.[18] The capacity of advisory opinions to develop international law as a means to protect and uphold community interest is even more evident when considering the novelty of climate-related proceedings.[19]

In 2023, two small-island states, Antigua and Barbuda (West Indies) and Tuvalu (Polynesia), adopted a treaty that established the Commission of Small Island States on Climate Change and International Law (COSIS).[20] This body submitted a request[21] for an advisory opinion to ITLOS, shedding light on the specific situation of climate-vulnerable states—whose survival is at stake[22]—and their willingness to induce compliance through international adjudication. The request aimed to clarify obligations of state parties to UNCLOS, specifically regarding the connection between climate change and the marine environment.[23]

Within the scope of these advisory proceedings, on May 21st 2024, ITLOS was the first international judicial body to deliver a climate-related advisory opinion. By participating in the proceedings through the submission of written statements, states presented their own narratives about climate change, reflecting their interests, values, and aspirations, in a manner to contribute to the discursive environment[24] around the issuance of the advisory opinion. Narratives can be defined as the organization of events, elements, and arguments in written or spoken form to

---

[17] *Responsibilities and Obligations of States Sponsoring Persons and Entities with Respect to Activities in the Area, Advisory Opinion, 1 February 2011, ITLOS Reports 2011, at 10.*, para 180.

[18] Cohen and Afogo (2023).

[19] There are two other climate-change-related requests for an advisory opinion before ICTs: Chile and Colombia, *Request for an Advisory Opinion on the Scope of the State Obligations for Responding to the Climate Emergency*, 1 September 2023, Inter-American Court of Human Rights, available at https://corteidh.or.cr/docs/opiniones/soc_1_2023_en.pdf; GA Res. 77/276, 4 April 2023.

[20] *About COSIS*, Commission of Small Island States on Climate Change and International Law, available at https://www.cosis-ccil.org/.

[21] Commission of Small Island States on Climate Change and International Law, *Request for Advisory Opinion*, 12 December 2022, International Tribunal for the Law of the Sea, available at https://www.itlos.org/fileadmin/itlos/documents/cases/31/Request_for_Advisory_Opinion_COSIS_12.12.22.pdf.

[22] Feria-Tinta (2023), 391.

[23] COSIS posed the following questions to the Tribunal: "What are the specific obligations of State Parties to the United Nations Convention on the Law of the Sea (the "UNCLOS"), including under Part XII: (a) to prevent, reduce and control pollution of the marine environment in relation to the deleterious effects that result or are likely to result from climate change, including through ocean warming and sea level rise, and ocean acidification, which are caused by anthropogenic greenhouse gas emissions into the atmosphere? (b) to protect and preserve the marine environment in relation to climate change impacts, including ocean warming and sea level rise, and ocean acidification?", see Commission of Small Island States on Climate Change and International Law, *supra* note 25.

[24] Miskimmon et al. (2012).

give them meaningful content[25] and persuade others in favour of the narrator's position.[26] States, as narrators, may craft texts and discourses with underlying political and national interests to influence how recipients perceive and behave concerning international affairs.[27] This process of deliberately creating narratives to advocate for a particular understanding of international law[28] operates and needs to be understood within a broader political context.

Assessing the narratives behind states' discourses and written submissions before ICTs, as well as the political context around them, is, thus, essential to understanding the crafting of states' 'foreign legal policy', which refers precisely to states' international legal actions based on their foreign policy interests, constituting a crucial key to the formation and interpretation of international law.[29] This approach reveals that international law often seeks a balance between the international community's ambitions and the individual states' practices and interests.[30] Beyond the idea that international law is only a body of rules and principles that determine the rights and obligations of the states,[31] there is also a prospective idea that it provides a framework and a vocabulary for international politics to occur. Despite the use of specialised vocabulary, words in the juridical domain possess significant relational value, and the meanings they encompass fluctuate in accordance with their accompanying terms.[32] The content of legal expressions varies with great frequency, so they should be understood in the context they are employed. This context contributes to the formation of narratives, which may be advanced before courts and tribunals and, consequently, are '*inseparably related*' to law.[33]

The assessment of narratives departs from the relation between law and linguistics since the technical legal lexicon has a deep connection with everyday language and shares its contradictions and ambiguities.[34] As international law texts are written, negotiated, interpreted and applied by people from different linguistic communities,[35] the power to interpret international norms remains highly dispersed.[36] Language and narratives are also a means to comprehend international law's 'historical contingencies' and how it is 'being represented'[37] according to specific

[25] Otten (2016), 196.

[26] Miskimmon et al. (2012).

[27] Wewerinke-Singh et al. (2023), 218.

[28] Otten (2016).

[29] de Lacharrière (2023).

[30] Klabbers (2023).

[31] Lowe (2012), 209.

[32] Focsaneanu (1970).

[33] Bianchi (2017).

[34] Focsaneanu (1970).

[35] Ibid.

[36] d'Aspremont (2012).

[37] Christensen (2021).

individual interests or identifiable groups' interests. The identifiable group examined in this research refers to the states comprised in the concept of Global South.

The expression 'Global South' emerged during the Cold War to outline inequalities in terms of states' development and to divert from the world division between capitalism and communism.[38] This term has remained relevant due to the historical and ongoing influence of politics and power across loosely defined geographical regions.[39] Consequently, the North-South divide reflects not merely a matter of location; since it represents unequal development and historical relations of economic and political dominance.[40] While acknowledging the heterogeneity of the states from the Global South, a common ground is found in shared colonial experiences and continued external influence, whose consequences extend over time and have resulted in inequalities in living standards, life expectancy, and access to resources. The legacy of colonialism is not only tied to the emergence of the term 'Global South' but is also closely linked to climate change's differentiated impacts. Conceptualised as 'colonially-driven environmental change', its root causes relate to the intersection between the political process of colonialization and economic development through capitalist industrial expansion.[41]

As narratives involve the organization of events and characters into meaningful and temporally oriented texts,[42] this book intends to capture the diverse positions of Global South states, shedding light on the broader political framework that shapes their engagement with climate-related issues. Under this context, it investigates whether states' narratives at ICTs are articulated with a broader political context, reflecting their interests expressed in other international arenas. Specifically, the book focuses on perceiving how, and with what aim, Global South states' narratives are articulated in the ITLOS advisory proceedings. Acknowledging the diversity within the Global South, the study investigates whether a shared history of colonialism and differing degrees of vulnerabilities to climate change inform cohesive narratives by the Global South within these proceedings. The objective is to identify and examine nuances, potential similarities or differences of narratives expressed through the legal arguments developed by Global South states at the ITLOS advisory proceedings[43] on climate change, in articulation with their

[38] Dados and Connell (2012).

[39] Schäfer and Peters (2021).

[40] Simma (1994) and Atapattu (2021).

[41] Whyte (2017).

[42] Zhao (2022).

[43] Eighteen Global South states submitted written statements: Brazil; China; Congo; Indonesia; Egypt; Chile; Bangladesh; Nauru; Belize; Guatemala; Sierra Leone; Micronesia; Djibouti; Rwanda; Vietnam; India; Mozambique; and Mauritius. See *Request for an Advisory Opinion Submitted by the Commission of Small Island States on Climate Change and International Law*, International Tribunal for the Law of the Sea, available at https://www.itlos.org/en/main/cases/list-of-cases/request-for-an-advisory-opinion-submitted-by-the-commission-of-small-island-states-on-climate-change-and-international-law-request-for-advisory-opinion-submitted-to-the-tribunal/.

political positions. Importantly, the comparative dimension of the research lies within the group of countries defined as 'Global South', rather than in between Global South and Global North states.

The choice of the Global South as a category of analysis is grounded in both the material and discursive asymmetries that shape international legal and political arenas. While heterogeneous in their economic, political, and geographic profiles, Global South states often share a legacy of colonial subjugation and structural marginalization in global governance. These commonalities are further exacerbated by the disproportionate impacts of climate change they endure, despite having contributed less to global emissions historically. This asymmetry reinforces a need for narratives that reflect demands for climate justice, historical responsibility, and equitable solutions. The selection of the ITLOS advisory proceedings as a focal point stems from its significance as the first international judicial body to issue an advisory opinion specifically addressing climate change. These proceedings thus offer a unique and timely forum to observe how Global South states construct their legal narratives in ways that are both responsive to their vulnerabilities and strategically positioned within political discourses.[44]

The book is therefore structured as follows: the first chapter is devoted to outlining the theoretical framework and defining the central concepts of the research, such as 'community interest', 'Global South', 'narratives', 'foreign legal policy', and 'strategy **(1)**'; the second chapter aims at identifying and describing the mixed-methodology designed to uncover state narratives before ICTs **(2)**; the third chapter examines qualitatively the political context surrounding Global South narratives on climate change, notably these states' political stances performed in multilateral arenas, comprised by the Conferences of the Parties (COPs) under the United Nations Framework Convention on Climate Change (UNFCCC) **(3)**; the fourth chapter investigates the Global South states' narratives in the ITLOS advisory proceedings on climate change expressed in their written and oral submissions via a combined quantitative-qualitative analysis through the categorical content analysis research technique[45] **(4)**; and the fifth chapter presents

---

[44] The ITLOS advisory proceedings were selected given the tribunal's status as the first international judicial body to issue an advisory opinion directly addressing climate change. Furthermore, several Global South states actively participated through written and oral submissions in these proceedings. This selection does not imply that the methodology developed for analysing narratives is inapplicable to other international courts or tribunals. On the contrary, future research intends to expand this analysis to the International Court of Justice (ICJ), including not only climate change-related proceedings but also broader cases concerning community interests. Although the Inter-American Court of Human Rights (IACHR) is a forum where Global South states are the main participants, it was not included within the current scope of analysis, given the study's focus on forums with broader state participation. Furthermore, ITLOS submissions are publicly available, ensuring transparency and accessibility for systematic analysis.

[45] R. Cardoso Sampaio and D. Lycarião, *Análise de Conteúdo Categorial: Manual de Aplicação* (2021).

a qualitative assessment that articulates the political positions adopted by Global South states at the COPs with the narratives advanced before the ITLOS during the cited proceedings **(5)**.

References

Atapattu S (2021) Global South Approaches. In: Rajamani L, Peel J (eds) The Oxford handbook of international environmental law, 2nd edn. 183

Benzing K (2006) Community interests in the procedure of international courts and tribunals. Law Pract Int Cts Tribun 5:369 at 371

Bianchi A (2017) International law theories. 294

Cardoso Sampaio R, Lycarião D (2021) Análise de Conteúdo Categorial: manual de Aplicação

Chayes A, Chayes AH (1998) The new sovereignty: compliance with international regulatory agreements. 209–210

Christensen LH (2021) Networks and Narrative: visualizing international law. Eur J Legal Stud

Cohen S, Afogo E (2023) The contribution of the International Tribunal for the Law of the Sea to the protection of human rights and the public interest at sea. PKI Glob Justice J 7

Commission of Small Island States on Climate Change and International Law (2022 Dec 12) Request for advisory opinion. International Tribunal for the Law of the Sea. Available at https://www.itlos.org/fileadmin/itlos/documents/cases/31/Request_for_Advisory_Opinion_COSIS_12.12.22.pdf

Cover RM (1983) The Supreme Court, 1982 Term—foreword: nomos and narrative. Fac Scholarsh Ser

d'Aspremont J (2012) Wording in international law. Leiden J Int'l L 575

Dados N, Connell R (2012) The global south. Contexts 11:12

de Lacharrière G (2023) La Politique Juridique Extérieure

Feria-Tinta C (2023) On the Request for an Advisory Opinion on Climate Change under UNCLOS before the International Tribunal for the Law of the Sea. J Int Dispute Settl 14:391

Focsaneanu C (1970) Les Langue Comme Moyen d'expression Du Droit International. Annuaire Français de Droit International 256

Gang (2022) The application of narrative research in international relations

Gray KR, Tarasofsky RG, Carlarne CT (2016) International Dispute Settlement. In: The Oxford handbook of international climate change law, 1 st edn. 418

Klabbers J (2023) International law, 4th edn

Klein N (2021) International environmental law disputes before international courts and tribunals. In: Rajamani L, Peel J, (eds) The Oxford handbook of international environmental law, 2nd edn. pp 1038–1052

Lowe V (2012) The function of litigation in international society. Int Comp L Q 61:209

Miskimmon A, O'Loughlin B, Roselle L (2012) Forging the world: strategic narratives and international relations

Otten (2016) Narratives in International Law. KritV, CritQ, RCrit, Kritische Vierteljahresschrift Für Gesetzgebung Und Rechtswissenschaft / Critical Quarterly for Legislation and Law / Revue Critique Trimestrielle de Jurisprudence et de Législation 99:187 at 196

Rajamani L, Peel J (eds) (2021) International environmental law disputes before international courts and tribunals. In: The Oxford handbook of international environmental law, 2nd edn. p 1039

Responsibilities and Obligations of States Sponsoring Persons and Entities with Respect to Activities in the Area, Advisory Opinion (2011 Feb 1) ITLOS Reports 2011 at 10. para 180

Schäfer R, Peters A (2021) Politics and the histories of international law: the quest for knowledge and justice

Simma B (1994) From bilateralism to community interest in international law. In: The Hague Academy Collected Courses Online/Recueil Des Cours de l'Académie de La Haye En Ligne, vol 250
Tanaka Y (2011) Protection of community interests in international law: the case of the law of the sea. Max Planck YB UN L Online 15:329
Von Bogdandy A, Venzke I (2011) On the democratic legitimation of international judicial lawmaking. Ger L J 12:1341
von Bogdandy A, Venzke I (2013) On the functions of international courts: an appraisal in light of their burgeoning public authority. Leiden J Int L 26:49
Von Bogdandy A, Venzke I (2011) Beyond dispute: international judicial institutions as law-makers. Ger L J 12:979
Wewerinke-Singh M, Viñuales JE, Aguon J (2023) The Role of Advocates in the Conception of Advisory Opinion Requests. AJIL Unbound 117:218–277
Whyte KP (2017) Indigenous climate change studies: indigenizing futures, decolonizing the Anthropocene. Engl Lang Notes 153
Wiik A (2018) Amicus curiae before international courts and tribunals. 505–506
Zimmermann A et al. (eds) (2019) The statute of the international court of justice: a commentary. 3rd edn. 361

Chapter 2
Understanding Core Concepts: A Theoretical Framework to Analyse States' Narratives

Abstract This chapter lays the conceptual groundwork for analysing how Global South states construct narratives in the advisory proceedings on climate change before the International Tribunal for the Law of the Sea (ITLOS). It explores how these narratives are strategically shaped by foreign legal policy and embedded within broader political contexts—particularly those reflected in non-judicial forums such as the COPs. The analysis identifies patterns of convergence and divergence among Global South submissions, linking them to the structural asymmetries and historical legacies of colonialism that continue to shape global climate governance. Central to this inquiry are five interrelated concepts: community interest, Global South, narratives, foreign legal policy, and strategy. Each of these is unpacked to clarify the analytical lens through which the legal and political engagement of Global South states is interpreted. By approaching international litigation as a site of strategic storytelling, the chapter highlights how legal discourse serves not only to defend national interests but also to influence the evolving meaning of global norms and public goods.

Keywords Community interest · Global South · Narratives · Foreign legal policy · Strategy

This research examines how Global South states construct their narratives in the ITLOS advisory proceedings on climate change, exploring how these narratives align with their political positions in non-judicial arenas—particularly the COPs. The goal is to identify patterns of affinity and divergence within this diverse group of states. By framing climate change as an issue of common concern and analysing modes of participation in international legal fora, the book contributes to a broader conceptualization of *community interests*. Given that the analysis focuses on the nuances of Global South narratives—despite their often-shared historical and structural conditions—clarifying the concepts of both *Global South* and *narratives*

P. Wojcikiewicz Almeida et al., *Uncovering Global South Narratives in ITLOS Advisory Proceedings on Climate Change*, SpringerBriefs in Law,
https://doi.org/10.1007/978-3-032-08427-9_2

becomes essential. These storylines do not arise in isolation; they are embedded within broader political contexts. Accordingly, the book considers how foreign policy ambitions shape the legal arguments presented by Global South states before the ITLOS, which requires engaging with the notions of *foreign legal policy* and *strategies*. This chapter clarifies the working definitions of the book's central concepts.

2.1 Community Interest

Traditionally, community interests refer to fundamental values that cannot be left entirely to the discretion of individual states, as they are recognized by international law as matters of concern for the international community as a whole.[1] This concept encompasses not only norms considered foundational—such as those with *jus cogens* status or obligations *erga omnes*—but also norms of lower hierarchical standing.[2] As such, community interests constitute a multilayered system of values, extending beyond rigid legal classifications or formal normative categories. At its core, the notion of community interest is closely linked to the nature of the object being regulated, as it aims to safeguard public goods and shared values that transcend national concerns, ultimately serving the collective interests of the international community.[3]

Despite ongoing debates regarding their definition and scope, community interests are widely recognized in international law.[4] They are often reflected in objectives that require collective legal action, such as the protection and creation of common goods, the preservation of shared spaces, and the pursuit of redistributive and intergenerational justice.[5] Illustrative examples include the maintenance of international peace and security, environmental protection, the safeguarding of humanity's common heritage, the promotion of human rights, and solidarity between developed and developing nations.[6] In some cases, obligations arising from diplomatic protection or international trade regimes may also reflect dimensions of community interest.[7] In sum, the concepts of community interests and common concern are closely tied to the notion of global public goods (GPGs), as both transcend individual state interests to protect values essential to the international community.[8]

[1] Feichtner (2007).

[2] Ibid.

[3] Benzing (2006).

[4] Wolfrum (2011).

[5] Almeida and Romay (2024).

[6] Almeida and Cohen (2023).

[7] Feichtner (2007).

[8] Benzing (2006).

Amid the growing recognition of community interests in international law, states engage in proceedings before international courts and tribunals where such issues are at stake. This involvement reflects an awareness that disputes concerning collective concerns transcend national boundaries and bear consequences for the global legal and political order. By taking part in these cases, states not only seek to advance their own interests but also play a role in shaping the normative frameworks that uphold shared values and protect collective goods essential to the international community.

2.2 Global South

The expression *Global South* emerged during the Cold War as a way to highlight disparities in development among states, offering an alternative framing to the binary division between capitalism and communism.[9] Its origins are closely tied to the concept of the Third World, with both terms referring to the challenges faced by states in achieving political and economic levels of development.[10] Over time, however, these terms came to represent alternative trajectories to both capitalism and socialism as pathways to modernity.[11] The continued relevance of the Global South lies in the enduring influence of political and economic power dynamics across loosely defined geographical regions.[12] Although the meaning and associated political agendas of the term have shifted considerably,[13] the North–South divide persists as more than a mere geographic distinction; it embodies systemic inequalities and longstanding patterns of economic and political dominance.[14] As such, the categories Global South and Global North should not be seen as fixed realities, but rather as constructs shaped through historical struggles between imperial domination and emancipatory resistance.[15]

While acknowledging the internal diversity of Global South states, a shared foundation can often be found in common colonial histories and the persistence of external influence, whose legacies have contributed to enduring disparities in living standards, life expectancy, and access to resources.[16] Colonialism's imprint is not only central to the emergence of the *Global South* as a concept, but also closely linked to the unequal impacts of climate change. Framed as 'colonially-driven environmental change', climate change uncovers disparities rooted in the

[9] Dados and Connell (2012).

[10] Dirlik (2007).

[11] Ibid.

[12] Schäfer and Peters (2021).

[13] Dirlik (2007) *h.*

[14] Dados and Connell (2012).

[15] Levander and Mignolo (2011) *h.*

[16] Dados and Connell (2012).

intersection of colonial political structures and capitalist industrial expansion.[17] In this context, the North–South divide is further deepened by the Global South's geographic vulnerability, limited regulatory capacity, and continued exploitation—ranging from the extraction of resources for Northern consumption and the relocation of polluting industries, to procedural injustices within global institutions dominated by Northern states.[18]

Despite its limitations in capturing the full complexity of states' internal inequalities,[19] the concept of the *Global South* remains a powerful analytical tool for examining global asymmetries, colonial legacies, and persistent power imbalances. Though its meaning has evolved beyond Cold War origins, the term continues to illuminate disparities in development, economic influence, and political representation. In an era of climate emergency, the heightened vulnerability of Global South countries underscores the lasting consequences of historical exploitation and economic inequities, reinforcing the term's continued relevance. The structural asymmetries between North and South also shape differing perspectives on international law[20]—differences that may be reflected in the narratives advanced by states before international courts and tribunals.

2.3 Narratives

Legal vocabulary, despite its specialised nature, carries significant relational value, with meanings that shift depending on the terms they accompany.[21] Hence, the content of legal expressions is fluid and must be interpreted within the specific settings in which they are used. This context is essential in shaping the narratives presented before courts and tribunals, rendering them '*inseparably related*' to law.[22] In the legal realm, the analysis of narratives emerges at the intersection of law and language, as legal terminology—despite its technical precision—is deeply rooted in ordinary language, sharing its inherent ambiguities and contradictions.[23] Legal narratology, as an interdisciplinary field, focuses on narratives *of* law and *within* law, examining how meaning is constructed, conveyed, and interpreted through legal discourses.[24]

To assess narratives *of* law, particularly the narrative forms through which law is presented to broader audiences,[25] the relationship between narrative and

---

[17] Whyte (2017) *s*.

[18] Gonzalez (2015) *w*.

[19] Kaltmeier (2015).

[20] Lorca (2023).

[21] Focsaneanu (1970).

[22] Cover (1983).

[23] Focsaneanu (1970).

[24] Pedersen (2025).

[25] Ibid.

normativity is central. Narratives can broadly be understood as sequences of causally linked events involving a finite number of characters and culminating in a shared outcome—whether describing real or imagined occurrences.[26] Norms, by contrast, prescribe, prohibit, or permit actions without necessarily narrating a specific situation.[27] Yet, by connecting events and characters, narratives can—under certain conditions—generate normative force, functioning as an interpretive lens through which their meaning is shaped.[28] The normative dimension of legal narratives is pivotal, as 'no set of legal institutions or prescriptions exists apart from the narratives that locate it and give it meaning'.[29] In this way, interpreting law through narrative reveals that the issuance or application of norms necessarily entails the construction of legal meaning through storytelling.[30]

Within this framework, '*law is narrative*'[31]—its coherence depends on a shared understanding of how legal stories generate meaning by linking characters and events within factual or fictional structures.[32] Legal narratology thus also includes narratives *in* law, focusing on how storytelling operates as a fundamental component of legal practice.[33] In this context, scholars investigate how stories are crafted and presented before courts and tribunals to frame legal arguments in particular directions. Jurists frequently rely on narrative forms to describe legal rules, convey their significance, and situate them historically.[34] Narrative, then, may be understood as a process of constructing meaning that allows individuals to make sense of reality. In formal legal venues such as courts and tribunals, narratives and counter-narratives compete to frame the legal relevance of people, actions, and events in distinct and often opposing ways.[35]

The study of legal narratives begins with the relationship between law and language,[36] and international legal mechanisms are written, negotiated, and applied by actors from diverse linguistic and cultural communities.[37] This diversity contributes to a decentralized interpretive authority in international law and provides fertile ground for narratological analysis—examining both narratives *of* and *in* international law. Narratives *of* international law explore the language and stories through which international law's historical contingencies and representations are

[26] Pfersmann (2019).

[27] Ibid.

[28] Ibid.

[29] Cover (1983) *v*.

[30] Ibid.

[31] Wharton and Miller (2016).

[32] Ibid.

[33] Pedersen (2025).

[34] Devinat (2016).

[35] Sari (2023).

[36] Focsaneanu (1970).

[37] Ibid.

articulated.[38] From this perspective, international law is not static but a discourse shaped by crises responding to them by the use of words.[39] Narratives *in* international law, by contrast, analyze the legal stories told by international legal actors in formal and informal adjudicatory settings.[40] Here, the international legal order is not seen merely as a system of abstract rules but as deeply shaped by the narratives constructed about it—narratives that influence how norms are understood, applied, and contested.[41] Narratives advanced before international courts and tribunals can thus produce legitimacy, promote particular values, and at times obscure or marginalize competing viewpoints.[42]

Narratives also involve organizing events and characters in a meaningful, temporally structured form, typically composed of three essential elements: the narrative material, the narrator, and the receiver.[43] Narrators in international law—such as states or political elites—use communicative tools to craft texts aimed at shaping how audiences interpret and respond to international affairs.[44] As such, narratives possess a strategic political function, serving as mechanisms through which states articulate their interests, project values, and influence the discursive environment around them, thereby shaping the dynamics of the international system.[45]

By highlighting the intrinsic relationship between language and law, narratology in the field of international legal scholarship reveals how narratives introduce an indispensable layer of meaning into legal discourse. They contribute to the evolving construction of the global legal order and mediate the interplay between facts, norms, and power. In this sense, narratives are powerful tools for asserting claims, legitimizing positions, and influencing decision-making. The analysis of foreign legal policy offers a productive bridge between narratological studies in international law and the field of strategic narratives. It investigates how states frame and perform legal arguments and discourse in global forums to advance their political objectives.

2.4 Foreign Legal Policy

The dynamics of international relations are significantly influenced by how states formulate and implement their legal strategies, often through differing interpretations of global and regional norms. The notion of *politique juridique*

---

[38] Christensen (2021).

[39] d'Aspremont (2022).

[40] Sari (2023) *V*.

[41] Lixinski (2013) *e*.

[42] Ibid.

[43] Gang (2022).

[44] Ibid.

[45] Miskimmon et al. (2012).

extérieure—or foreign legal policy—captures how national interests shape states' engagement with international law, emphasizing that legal considerations in foreign policy are intertwined with political objectives, even when not explicitly stated.[46] In this regard, foreign legal policy refers to the judicial and legal strategies deployed by states to promote their interests on the international stage, recognizing that such actions are not always governed by a strict commitment to legal norms.[47] This does not equate to a complete disregard for international law, but rather reflects how states routinely recalibrate their external practices in response to shifting interests, occasionally drawing on ambiguities in legal texts.[48] Consequently, international law emerges as a flexible tool that can be deployed for political purposes—a feature particularly relevant in the context of the Global South's longstanding criticisms of traditional interpretations of international law.

States develop their legal positions in international affairs primarily with the aim of safeguarding national interests, often managing international norms in ways that align legal outcomes with broader political agendas.[49] While international legal obligations are rarely ignored, they are selectively mobilized, shaped by both constraints and opportunities, to serve the foreign policy aims of individual states.[50] Hence, as previously outlined, examining a country's foreign legal policy does not entail denying the normative presence of international law or asserting its supremacy; rather, it underscores the practical dimension of law as interpreted and mobilized by states either to legitimize their conduct or to avoid unfavorable consequences.

Importantly, the concept of foreign legal policy should not be conflated with 'foreign relations law', which typically concerns the domestic regulation of external affairs.[51] In contrast, *politique juridique extérieure* focuses on how states strategically engage with international law to advance their national interests.[52] Here, international law is not merely a set of obligations to be met, but also a political language and structure through which states can shape, contest, and assert influence over global norms.[53] It reflects a continual negotiation between the ideals of the international community and the pragmatic interests of individual states.[54] Beyond the idea that international law is only a body of rules and

[46] de Lacharrière (1983).

[47] Ibid.

[48] Ibid.

[49] Cazala (2013).

[50] Ibid.

[51] For a more in-depth discussion on Foreign Relations Law see Aust and Kleinlein (eds), *Encounters between Foreign Relations Law and International Law: Bridges and Boundaries* (Cambridge University Press Mégret 2021).

[52] Mégret (2021).

[53] Ibid.

[54] Klabbers (2020).

principles that determine the rights and obligations of the states,[55] there is also a prospective idea that it provides a framework and a vocabulary for international politics to occur.

Thus, studying *politique juridique extérieure* challenges the notion of international law as an autonomous, apolitical system. It presents a more nuanced understanding of law as both a constraint and a resource—deployed strategically to serve national agendas—highlighting the entangled relationship between legal norms and geopolitical realities. Nevertheless, any analysis of foreign legal policy must also account for states' confidence in international courts and tribunals, their willingness to participate in global legal processes, and the influence of other critical actors such as non-governmental organizations, transnational corporations, and academic discourse on international law.[56]

2.5 Strategy

Climate change litigation in international law is often read through the lens of strategic action.[57] In this context, strategic litigation refers to efforts primarily aimed at influencing laws, policies, or systemic patterns of governmental and corporate behavior.[58] Such litigation also serves to raise public awareness and mobilize broader support for specific causes.[59] The decision to pursue litigation often involves balancing between taking the case to court and using alternative approaches, such as advocacy, to achieve efficiently and promptly specific goals—including promoting structural reforms and implementing domestic policies.[60] Civil society organizations, namely NGOs, tend to play a key role in promoting strategic litigation through amicus curiae and/or third-party interventions.[61]

When approached expansively—as this research proposes—virtually any case can be viewed as 'strategic' insofar as it seeks to enhance the litigant's leverage *vis-à-vis* the opposing party.[62] Early academic work on the topic often centered on case-specific impacts or examined the motivations behind state-led litigation before international courts. For example, the Military and Paramilitary Activities in and against Nicaragua case (Nicaragua v. United States of America) has been studied in terms of how parties used the International Court of Justice to advance political and

[55] Lowe (2012).

[56] Pellet (1985); Alland (2012).

[57] Meguro (2020); Peel and Lin (2019); Rodríguez-Garavito (2022); Sindico et al (2024); Stephens (2014).

[58] Rose et al (2024).

[59] Ibid.

[60] Huneeus (2015).

[61] Hondora (2018).

[62] Fischer-Lescano (2021).

diplomatic objectives.[63] In this light, developing an effective litigation strategy involves considering a range of interrelated elements, including the legal team involved, the rationale for pursuing litigation, and the strengths and vulnerabilities of the case itself.[64]

Strategic litigation extends beyond the deployment of legal arguments; it often entails the deliberate construction of narratives that frame facts and events to serve the political and legal interests of the actor. States craft such narratives to influence institutional perceptions and outcomes within international courts and tribunals, where divergent stories compete for the attention and endorsement of judges or other relevant actors.[65] Through these narratives, states seek not only to justify their conduct but also to shape the interpretive environment of international law, signaling their identity, normative preferences, and visions of global order.[66] These stories are inherently future-oriented: they rely on interpretations of past and present events to articulate desired futures and to reshape existing legal and political arrangements.[67]

Building on this discussion, the present work aims to examine how Global South states have strategically advanced their narratives before the ITLOS's advisory proceedings on climate change and how these narratives form an integral part of their foreign legal policy. By analyzing their use of storytelling, the study seeks to uncover how these states not only defend their immediate interests but also may project a vision of their national and/or regional interests, contributing to the broader redefinition of international norms and structures. This approach sheds light on the ways Global South countries engage with the international legal system—not merely as passive participants, but as active agents shaping the global order to reflect their strategic priorities and long-term aspirations.

References

About the Secretariat (UNFCCC) https://unfccc.int/about-us/about-the-secretariat. Accessed 16 Oct 2024

Alland D (2012) Quelques observations sur la notion de politique juridique de l'État. Annuaire Français de Relations Internationales 13

Almeida PW, Romay GT (2024) Expanding access to justice: an empirical analysis of the participation of state and non-state actors in the international court of justice. Springer

---

[63] Rijpkema (1990).

[64] Pellet and Barsac (2019).

[65] Nurse (2019).

[66] Miskimmon, O'Loughlin and Roselle, *Forging the World: Strategic Narratives and International Relations* (University of Michigan Press Miskimmon et al. 2012).

[67] Gang, 'The Application of Narrative Research in International Relations' in *Proceedings of the 2022 3rd International Conference on Language, Art and Cultural Exchange* (Atlantis Press He Gang 2022) 258–261.

Almeida P, Cohen M (2023) Mapping the "public" in public interest litigation: an empirical analysis of participants before the international court of justice. In: Bendel J and Suedi Y (eds) Public interest litigation in international law, Routledge

Benzing K (2006) Community interests in the procedure of international courts and tribunals. Law Pract Int Court Trib 5

Berlin Climate Change Conference (1995) (UNFCCC) https://unfccc.int/conference/berlin-climate-change-conference-march-1995#documents. Accessed 16 Oct 2024

Cardoso Sampaio R, Lyciarão D (2021) Análise de Conteúdo Categorial: manual de Aplicação. Enap

Cazala B (2013) Retour sur un classique: guy de Lacharrière, La politique juridique extérieure. Rgdip 2:6

Christensen ML (2021) Networks and narrative: visualizing international law. Eur J Leg Stud

Cover RM (1983) Foreword: nomos and narrative. Harv L Rev 97

Dados N, Connell R (2012) The global south. Contexts 11(1):12. https://doi.org/10.1177/1536504212436479

d'Aspremont B (2022) International law as a crisis discourse: the peril of wordlessness. In: d'Aspremont B, Mbengue MM (eds) Crisis narratives in international law, 1st edn. Brill

Devinat G (2016) Réflexion Sur La Narration Judiciaire Dans Les Jugements De La Cour Suprême Du Canada. Cahiers de Méthodologie Juridique 30

Dirlik A (2007) Global south: predicament and promise. Glob South 1(1)

Feichtner K (2007) Community interest. In: Wolfrum R, (ed) Max planck encyclopedia of public international law. Oxford University Press

Fischer-Lescano A (2021) From strategic litigation to juridical action. In Saage-Maaß M, Zumbansen P, Bader M, Shahab P (eds) Transnational legal activism in global value chains: The Ali Enterprises factory fire and the struggle for justice, Springer, pp. 299–312. https://doi.org/10.1007/978-3-030-73835-8_15

Focsaneanu D (1970) Les Langue Comme Moyen d'expression Du Droit International. Annuaire Français de Droit International

Gang (2022) The application of narrative research in international relations. In: 3rd International Conference on Language, Art and Cultural Exchange ICLACE, Advances in social science, education and humanities research, vol 673. Atlantis Press

Gang H (2022) The application of narrative research in international relations. In: Proceedings of the 2022 3rd international conference on language, art and cultural exchange. Atlantis Press, pp 258–261

Gehring T, Spielmann L (2023) The treaty management organization established under the UNFCCC and the paris agreement: an international actor in its own right? Int Environ Agreem Polit Law Econ 23:235

Gonzalez CG (2015) Environmental justice, human rights, and the global south. Santa Clara J Int Law 13

Hondora T (2018) Civil society's role in the development of international law through strategic litigation in challenging times. SSRN Electr J. https://doi.org/10.2139/ssrn.3262661

Huneeus A (2015) Reforming the state from afar: Structural reform litigation at the human rights courts. Yale J Int Law 40(1):1–40

Kaltmeier O (2015) Global South. Concepts of Global South (1). University of Cologne Global South Studies Center. https://gssc.uni-koeln.de/sites/BiPoN/user_upload/7_GLOBAL_SOUTH_voices012015_concepts_of_the_global_south_Kopie.pdf

Klabbers J (2020) The subjects of international law. In: International law, Cambridge University Press

Lacharrière G de (1983) La Politique Juridique Extérieure. Économica

Levander C, Mignolo WD (2011) Introduction: the global south and world dis/order. Glob South 5(1)

Lixinski L (2013) Narratives of the international legal order and why they matter. ELR June

Lorca A (2023) After TWAIL's success, what next? Afterword to the foreword. Eur J Int Law 34(4)

Lowe V (2012) The function of litigation in international society. ICLQ 61
Mayring P (2020) Qualitative content analysis: demarcation, varieties, developments. Forum Qual Soz/Forum Qual Soc Res Art 20(3):16. https://dx.doi.org/10.17169/fqs-20.3.3343
Mégret F (2021) Foreign legal policy as the background to foreign relations law? Revisiting guy de Lacharrière's La politique juridique extérieure. In: Aust HP, Kleinlein T (eds) Encounters between foreign relations law and international law: bridges and boundaries, Cambridge University Press
Meguro M (2020) Litigating climate change through international law: Obligations strategy and rights strategy. Leid J Int Law 33(4):933–951. https://doi.org/10.1017/S0922156520000473
Miskimmon A, O'Loughlin B, Roselle L (2012) Forging the world: strategic narratives and international relations. University of Michigan Press
Nurse A (2019) Law, the environment and narrative. In: Creutzfeldt N et al (eds) Routledge Handbook of Socio-Legal Theory and Methods, 1st edn. Routledge, p. 301
Pedersen FH (2025) Narratives in court decisions. In: Spoo R et al (eds) Elgar concise encyclopedia of law and literature, Edward Elgar Publishing
Peel J, Lin J (2019) Transnational Climate Litigation: The Contribution of the Global South. Am J Int Law 113(4):679–726. https://doi.org/10.1017/ajil.2019.48
Pellet A (1985) Le Sage, le Prince et le Savant (À propos de La politique juridique extérieure de Guy de Lacharrière). J du Droit International 2:1128
Pellet A, Barsac T (2019) Litigation strategy. In Max Planck Encyclopaedia of International Procedural Law (MPEiPro), Oxford University Press. https://doi.org/10.1093/law-mpeipro/e3109.013.3109
Pfersmann O (2019) Le Droit Est-Il Narratif, La Narrativité Est-Elle Juridique? Revue Droit and Littérature 3
Rijpkema PP (1990) T.D. Gill Litigation Strategy at the International Court A Case Study of the Nicaragua v. United States Dispute M. Nijhoff Publ Dordrecht 1989 XV + 362 pp. Dfl. 175/$ 95/£ 56. Netherlands Int Law Rev 37(02):278–279. https://doi.org/10.1017/S0165070X00006586
Rodríguez-Garavito C (ed) (2022) Litigating the climate emergency: How human rights, courts, and legal mobilization can bolster climate action. Cambridge University Press. https://doi.org/10.1017/9781009106214
Rose A, Mladenova D, Newman V (2024) The crucial role of strategic climate litigation. In Law 2024, pp. 18–36. https://doi.org/10.4337/9781800889781.00008
Sari A (2023) Norm contestation for strategic effect: legal narratives as information advantage. ZaöRV 83
Sarica S, Luo J (2021) Stopwords in technical language processing. PLOS ONE 16:e0254937. https://journals.plos.org/plosone/article?id=10.1371/journal.pone.0254937. Accessed 1 October 2024
Schäfer R, Peters A (2021) Politics and the histories of international law: the quest for knowledge and justice. Brill Nijhoff
Sindico F, McKenzie K, Medici-Colombo G, Wegener L (eds) (2024) Research Handbook on Climate Change Litigation
Stephens T (2014) International environmental disputes: to sue or not to sue? In: Klein N, (ed) Litigating International Law Disputes: Weighing the Options, Chapter, Cambridge: Cambridge University Press, pp. 284–304
Whyte KP (2017) Indigenous climate change studies: indigenizing futures, decolonizing the anthropocene. Eng Lang Notes 55
Wharton R, Miller D (2016) New directions in law and narrative. Law Cult Humanit 15(2)
What Is the United Nations Framework Convention on Climate Change? UNFCCC. Available at https://unfccc.int/process-and-meetings/what-is-the-united-nations-framework-convention-on-climate-change.
Wolfrum R (2011) Enforcing community interests through international dispute settlement: reality or utopia? In: Fastenrath U et al (eds) From bilateralism to community interest: essays in honour of judge bruno simma, Oxford University Press

Chapter 3
Unlocking State Narratives Before ICTs: A Mixed-Method Approach

Abstract This chapter presents the methodological approach adopted to examine how Global South states constructed their narratives in the ITLOS advisory proceedings on climate change. By combining qualitative and quantitative techniques—particularly categorical content analysis—it investigates the written and oral submissions of eighteen Global South states that participated in the ITLOS advisory proceedings on climate change. Rather than comparing these to Global North submissions, the study emphasizes within-group variation to uncover how legal arguments reflect differing political priorities and strategic objectives. The method includes mapping participation, contextualizing narratives through high-level UNFCCC COP statements, and conducting an inductive analysis of six legal categories. These categories were then linked to political discourses to identify two overarching narratives: one centred on developmental concerns, and the other on existential vulnerability.

Keywords Categorical content analysis · Global South · Narratives · International legal strategy

As narratives involve the organization of events and characters into meaningful and temporally oriented texts,[1] this book aims at assessing the narratives presented by Global South states in both their written and oral submissions to the ILTOS advisory proceedings on climate change mainly through the categorical

[1] Gang He (2022), 258–261.

Natália Barcelos, PhD Candidate in Sociology at the Institute of Social and Political Studies, State University of Rio de Janeiro (IESP-UERJ), is a contributing author to this chapter.

P. Wojcikiewicz Almeida et al., *Uncovering Global South Narratives in ITLOS Advisory Proceedings on Climate Change*, SpringerBriefs in Law,
https://doi.org/10.1007/978-3-032-08427-9_3

content analysis research technique.[2] By focusing our analysis on the Global South—and recognizing the internal heterogeneity that characterizes it—this study is primarily concerned with exploring the *within-group* variation among Global South states narratives, rather than drawing *between-group* comparisons with the Global North ones, which were not included in our empirical corpus.[3] The use of categorical content analysis as a methodological tool offers valuable insights into how narratives are constructed and expressed, particularly in contexts where similar terms may carry diverse meanings.[4] This technique facilitates the systematic examination of textual, oral and\or imagistic data, enabling the identification of recurring elements and the interpretation of underlying meaning patterns.[5] Thus, categorical content analysis serves as a critical method for uncovering the nuances of legal arguments. By analysing narratives, the authors intend to capture the diverse interpretations and positions of states, shedding light on the broader political framework that shapes their engagement with climate-related issues.

The assessment of the narratives addressed by Global South states in their written and oral submissions was conducted in four distinct but complementary phases, including both quantitative and qualitative techniques. Following a literature review to establish the theoretical framework and to define key concepts applied in the research (see Chap. 1), the methodology included: mapping the participation of states, in general, and of Global South states, in particular, in the ITLOS advisory proceedings on climate change (3.1); a qualitative examination of the political context from which the narratives presented by Global South states in the ITLOS advisory proceedings arise (3.2); a combined quantitative-qualitative inquiry of legal arguments through categorical content analysis of written and oral submissions of Global South states during the cited advisory proceedings (3.3), and a qualitative analysis of the categorised content in relation to the political context surrounding it (3.4).

[2] This research did not apply the 'Narrative Analysis' method, which requires the examination of a narrative in three basic steps, namely: 'formation', 'projection' and 'reception' (Miskimmon et al. 2012). The first of these steps, represented by 'formation', is similar to the analysis of political context proposed in this research; but it is connected to the subsequent steps, which focus on understanding the specific identity of the narrative's authors and their strategy for influencing the international landscape. In contrast, this research adopts a different methodological approach, concentrating on the narratives presented in courts and tribunals (specifically in the ITLOS). While the political context is still considered, this research did not address its potential impacts on identity and strategy.

[3] To a broader justification of Global South as a category of analysis, see *Introduction*.

[4] Mayring P (2020) 20(3).

[5] Cardoso Sampaio R. and Lyciarão D (2021).

3.1 Mapping Global South Participation in ITLOS Advisory Proceedings on Climate Change

The initial methodological step consists of a quantitative analysis of state and institutional participation in the ITLOS advisory proceedings on climate change. In total, 34 state parties to the United Nations Convention on the Law of the Sea (UNCLOS) submitted written statements under the Article 133(1) of the ITLOS Rules of the Tribunal. Additionally, nine international organizations contributed to the proceedings.[6] This participation is grounded in Article 133(2), which authorizes the Tribunal to invite international organizations likely to offer relevant information, and Article 84(2), which permits such organizations to submit information on their own initiative. Although the ITLOS framework does not provide for the formal participation of non-state actors—including NGOs and academic institutions—a total of ten such actors submitted written statements.[7] However, these were not incorporated into the official case file.

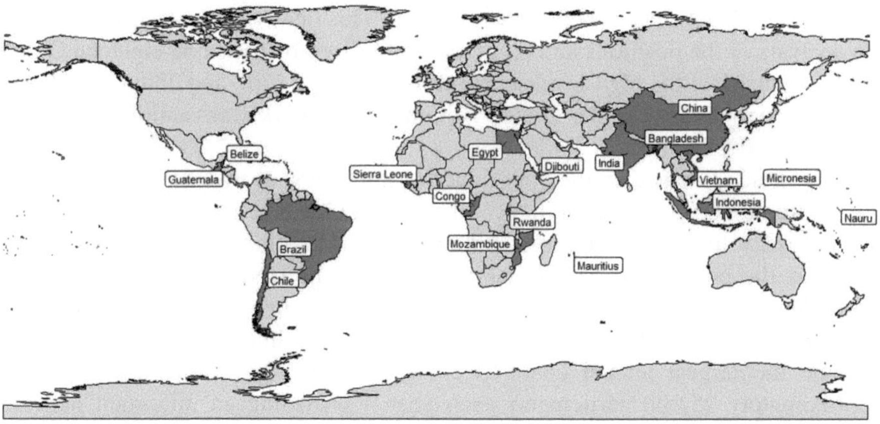

Fig. 3.1 Global South states: Written Statements Marked on the World Map. *Source* Authors; data collected from the ITLOS website

---

[6] The International Organizations invited to submit their considerations on the case were United Nations, International Union for the Conservation of Nature (IUCN), International Maritime Organization (IMO), Commission of Small Island States on Climate Change and International Law (COSIS), Pacific Community (SPC), United Nations Environment Programme (UNEP), African Union, International Seabed Authority (ISA), and Food and Agricultural Organization of the United Nations (FAO).

[7] United Nations Special Rapporteurs on Human Rights & Climate Change, Toxics & Human Rights and Human Rights & the Environment, High Seas Alliance, ClientEarth, Opportunity Green, Center for International Environmental Law (CIEL) and Greenpeace International, Advisory Committee on Protection of the Sea (ACOPS), World Wide Fund for Nature (WWF), Our Children's Trust and Oxfam International, Observatory for Marine and Coastal Governance, One Ocean Hub.

The analysis of this book focuses on the eighteen Global South states that issued written statements in the advisory proceedings on climate change, namely: Bangladesh, Belize, Brazil, Chile, China, Congo, Djibouti, Egypt, Guatemala, India, Indonesia, Mauritius, Micronesia, Mozambique, Nauru, Rwanda, Sierra Leone, and Vietnam (Fig. 3.1). In addition to the analysis of these written submissions, the book also examines the oral statements from the same states, with the exception of Brazil, Egypt, and Rwanda, which did not deliver oral interventions.

3.2 Qualitative Analysis of the Political Context Underlying Narratives Presented by Global South States

The second step focuses on tracing relevant political positions of the Global South states involved in these advisory proceedings. Considering that narratives result from broader conditions which enable their emergence, the goal of this stage is to underpin the underlying political context that might have led Global South states to adopt certain legal stances before the Tribunal. This objective was fulfilled through the analysis of the positions and arguments mobilised by the same eighteen Global South countries at the high-level segments of the 26th, 27th, and 28th Conferences of the Parties (COPs) to the United Nations Framework Convention on Climate Change (UNFCCC).

This choice is based on the importance of the COPs, as they may be considered the 'supreme decision-making body' of the UNFCCC,[8] whose primary goal is to prevent risky human interference within the world's climate system. The COPs serves as the principal decision-making forum of the UNFCCC agreement.[9] The first COP took place in Berlin in 1995 and marked the beginning of the debates on the implementation of the UNFCCC's resolutions.[10] Since then, the COPs have become the largest annual conference organised by the United Nations, with approximately 25,000 participants each year,[11] providing an important platform for multilateral negotiations on climate change.[12] The importance of the COPs may also be reflected in the fact that the Commission of Small Island States on Climate Change and International Law (COSIS), which is the requesting body of the ITLOS advisory opinion on climate change, was created exactly during the preparatory discussions for the COP 26.

[8] *What Is the United Nations Framework Convention on Climate Change?* UNFCCC. Available at https://unfccc.int/process-and-meetings/what-is-the-united-nations-framework-convention-on-climate-change.

[9] Gehring and Spielmann (2023).

[10] 'Berlin Climate Change Conference—March 1995' (UNFCCC) https://unfccc.int/conference/berlin-climate-change-conference-march-1995#documents accessed 16 October 2024.

[11] 'About the Secretariat' (UNFCCC) https://unfccc.int/about-us/about-the-secretariat accessed 16 October 2024.

[12] Kaya and Schofield (2020).

The analysis of the political context under which the narratives were crafted included the following COPs: (i) COP 26 (Glasgow, 2021); (ii) COP 27 (Sharm-el-Sheikh, 2022); and (iii) COP 28 (Abu Dhabi, 2023). Specifically, this research focused on the high-level segments, since they represent the main venue in which heads of government and other high-level state representatives give statements about their countries' perspectives on climate change.[13] In This context, the eighteen Global South countries that issued written statements to the ITLOS advisory proceedings on climate change issued a total of 54 speeches in the COPs 26, 27, and 28. Most speeches are accessible on the official UNFCCC website.[14] Nonetheless, some were only available on the website of the Ministries of Foreign Affairs and Environment of the states.[15]

After gathering the information on these political statements, their content were categorised into two main themes: *Inequalities Between States* and *Development and Sustainability*. This choice reflects the identification of certain trends in the statements of Global South states and bears correspondence with the relevance and

[13] University of Connecticut, 'What is the UN COP Climate Change Conference?' https://sustainability.uconn.edu/what-is-the-un-cop-climate-change-conference/ accessed 20 September 2024.

[14] UNFCCC, 'Home' (2024) https://unfccc.int/ accessed 3 October 2024.

[15] **Regarding COP 26:** Carlos Agostinho do Rosário, 'Discurso Da S.Exa. Primeiro-Ministro de Moçambique Na Abertura Da COP26' (November 2021) https://mozambique.un.org/pt/157254-discurso-da-sexa-primeiro-ministro-de-mo%C3%A7ambique-na-abertura-da-cop26 accessed 17 September 2024. **Regarding COP 27:** Joaquim Leite, 'Somos parte da solução' (Ministério do Meio Ambiente, 15 September 2024) https://www.gov.br/mma/pt-br/assuntos/noticias/somos-parte-da-solucao-diz-ministro-em-discurso-na-conferencia-do-clima accessed 17 September 2024; Arab Republic of Egypt Presidency, 'President El-Sisi's Speech at the Opening Session of COP 27' (7 November 2022) https://www.sis.gov.eg/Story/172566/President-El-Sisi's-Speech-at-the-Opening-Session-of-COP-27?lang=en-us accessed 17 September 2024. **Regarding COP 28:** Abdel Fattah Al Sisi, 'President El-Sisi's Speech at UN Climate Change Conference COP28' (COP28 High-Level Segment Statement, November 2023) https://www.sis.gov.eg/Story/190337/President-El-Sisi accessed 17 September 2024; Joko Widodo, 'Remarks of President of the Republic of Indonesia at the COP28 Presidency Session at Al Waha Theatre, Expo City Dubai, Dubai, the United Arab Emirates, December 2, 2023' (COP28 High-Level Segment Statement, 2 December 2023) https://setkab.go.id/en/remarks-of-president-of-the-republic-of-indonesia-at-the-cop28-presidency-session-at-al-waha-theatre-expo-city-dubai-dubai-the-united-arab-emirates-december-2-2023/ accessed 17 September 2024; Maria-Heloísa Rojas, 'COP28 Summit 2023 LIVE: Second Part of the High-Level Summit Kicks off at COP28' (COP28 High-Level Segment Statement, 9 December 2023) https://www.youtube.com/watch?v=6epub1n2B-Q accessed 17 September 2024; Shahab Uddin, 'COP28 Summit 2023 LIVE: Second Part of the High-Level Summit Kicks off at COP28' (COP28 High-Level Segment Statement, 9 December 2023) https://www.youtube.com/watch?v=6epub1n2B-Q accessed 17 September 2024; Jeanne d'Arc Mujawamariya, 'NATIONAL STATEMENT—COP28 UN Climate Change Conference' (COP28 High-Level Segment Statement, 2023) https://climatechange.gov.rw/index.php?id=35&tx_news_pi1%5Bnews%5D=449&tx_news_pi1%5Bcontroller%5D=News&tx_news_pi1%5Baction%5D=detail&cHash=4a951bb35bac1de2b48084a2a32f6b1f#:~:text=Rwanda%2C%20as%20Commonwealth%20Chair%2Din accessed 17 September 2024. These statements were not available on the UNFCCC's official website.

frequency according to which these topics were mentioned across various high-level statements issued in the analysed COPs. Regarding the first category (*Inequalities Between States*), multiple states have positioned themselves as belonging to particularly vulnerable groups seeking cooperation and funding for mitigation and adaptation efforts. Identifying themselves as vulnerable, other states frequently mentioned their developmental priorities, taking into account climate change and the demand for sustainable development. The second category (*Development and Sustainability*) refers to this dual dilemma faced by Global South states: advancing economic development while confronting the realities of climate change.

3.3 Mixed-Method Analysis of the Narratives Presented by Global South States in Their Submissions to the ITLOS Advisory Opinion on Climate Change

The third stage of the research comprises the analysis of the written and oral submissions issued by Global South states in the referred advisory proceedings via categorical content analysis. The 'categorical content analysis' is a research technique that aims to examine written, spoken and imagistic communication tools for describing, quantifying, and interpreting the meanings within them.[16] Applying such a technique allows the identification of potential similarities and differences in the arguments advanced before the Tribunal to uncover narratives along with divergent viewpoints. In this stage, the categorical content analysis comprised the following intertwined steps:

3.3.1 Qualitative Approach

The qualitative approach consisted of the inductive reading of the submissions addressed by Global South states, as available in PDF format at the ITLOS's official website,[17] to identify the most frequently mobilised topics. The authors initially conducted a first round of readings to identify the most frequently addressed themes across the written submissions. Based on this preliminary analysis, they proceeded with further rounds of close reading to refine the identification of analytical categories

---

[16] Cardoso Sampaio R. and Lyciarão D (2021).

[17] Request for an Advisory Opinion submitted by the Commission of Small Island States on Climate Change and International Law (Request for Advisory Opinion submitted to the Tribunal). https://www.itlos.org/en/main/cases/list-of-cases/request-for-an-advisory-opinion-submitted-by-the-commission-of-small-island-states-on-climate-change-and-international-law-request-for-advisory-opinion-submitted-to-the-tribunal/ accessed 20 September 2024.

and locate the specific excerpts in which these categories appeared in each submission. After each round, the authors held meetings to align and adjust the criteria for identifying and interpreting each category, ensuring consistency and accuracy throughout the analysis.

Through this iterative and collaborative process, six categories were inductively identified: (i) Jurisdiction, (ii) Principle of Common but Differentiated Responsibilities, (iii) Duties of Cooperation and Assistance, (iv) Obligation to Prevent Pollution of the Marine Environment, (v) Human Rights, and (vi) Remedies. These categories functioned as analytical tools for capturing convergences and divergences in meaning, emphasis, and legal positioning within the submissions. Importantly, the process of categorising the content of the submissions was not restricted to identifying or quantifying the exact expressions corresponding to the titles of the selected categories, nor to cataloguing the sources of international law cited in each statement. Rather, the method adopted involved a comprehensive analysis of the full argumentative content, aiming to inductively identify categories through qualitative interpretation. To ensure the scientific robustness and falsifiability of the research, this interpretative process was guided by clearly defined criteria.[18] These criteria are further detailed in the following chapter.

3.3.2 *Quantitative Approach*

The quantitative part of the categorical content analysis employed Natural Language Processing (NLP) techniques to conduct a descriptive analysis of the relevant submissions.[19] To apply NLP, two distinct stages were considered: (i) data collection and (ii) pre-processing. Data collection involved the gathering of the states' written submissions in PDF format from the ITLOS's official website.[20] The collected PDF documents were pre-processed by applying R programming language to create a database containing the complete content of each submission, the file identifier, and the author of the document (*i.e.*, state). The texts of the

[18] Mayring (2020).

[19] NLP involves computational methods that allow computers to understand and process human language. Thus, it is possible for the computer to examine the structure, meanings, contexts, and relations between words in a given text. In addition to processing textual content, NLP also enables predictions and visual and descriptive analyses. For more information on the NLP technique, see: Ng and Zelle, 'Corpus-Based Approaches to Semantic Interpretation in NLP', 18 *AI Mag.* (1997) 45.

[20] Request for an Advisory Opinion submitted by the Commission of Small Island States on Climate Change and International Law (Request for Advisory Opinion submitted to the Tribunal). https://www.itlos.org/en/main/cases/list-of-cases/request-for-an-advisory-opinion-submitted-by-the-commission-of-small-island-states-on-climate-change-and-international-law-request-for-advisory-opinion-submitted-to-the-tribunal/ accessed 20 September 2024.

submissions were then *normalised,*[21] and *stopwords*[22]—articles, prepositions, punctuation, conjunctions, and pronouns—were removed. After this, a column with the total word count of each submission was added to the database.

The pre-processing also comprised term co-occurrence and word counting, without including predictions or sentiment analysis. Using the submissions database (Database A), this research calculated the co-occurrence of terms, *i.e.*, words appearing together in the same document or in the same sentence. First, a *corpus*[23] was created from Database A; and then the *tokenization*[24] was applied, which allowed the submissions' texts to be divided into logical units used to build the grammatical structure of the texts. The co-occurrence of terms was calculated based on a matrix containing the frequency of terms in the documents, or document-feature matrix (DFM). Within the tokenization, it was possible to construct the DFM and calculate the co-occurrence of terms using the *textplot_network*[25] function from the *quanteda*[26] package in R.

In addition, a second database gathering the arguments extracted from the archives of each submission was created, and their content was manually divided into six categories.[27] After the categorisation, the.docx files of each category were transformed into another database (Database B) by using the same method applied to Database A. Database B also contains information about the author of the submission, the category to which the argument belongs, and the content of the argument. *Normalisation* and the removal of *stopwords* were applied to enable the calculation of the total word-count of the arguments employed by the states in each category. By using the author-column present in

[21] Text normalisation is the process of standardisation, in which transformations (such as converting all letters to lowercase; removing extra spaces, accents, and punctuation; and replacing variant terms with a single form) are applied. The goal is to reduce variations that do not add meaning to the content, making automatic text analysis easier.

[22] We refer to stopwords as non-informative words, that is, words that do not add much to the meaning of a text and, therefore, should be removed during preprocessing to improve the quality of textual data analysis (Serhad Sarica and Jianxi Luo, 'Stopwords in Technical Language Processing' (2021) 16 PLOS ONE e0254937 <https://journals.plos.org/plosone/article?id=10.1371/journal.pone.0254937> accessed 1 October 2024.).

[23] A Corpus is a collection of real texts, often including transcripts of spoken language, that can be processed by computers (Tony McEnery, Richard Xiao and Yukio Tono, *Corpus-Based Language Studies: An Advanced Resource Book* (Taylor & Francis 2006)). It is designed to represent a specific language or variety of languages.

[24] Tokenization is the process of breaking text into smaller units for analysis. These units can be words, groups of words, or even entire sentences. The text can be split into different levels such as characters, words, sentences, lines or paragraphs.

[25] Function for visualising textual data, where the edges show co-occurrences of features. https://quanteda.io/reference/textplot_network.html.

[26] Quantitative Analysis of Textual Data: https://quanteda.io/index.html.

[27] Researchers categorised the content of the submissions from a group of states and selected the complete argument corresponding to one of the categories, including footnotes, in a .docx document.

both databases, the proportion of words in a specific category was calculated in relation to the total word-count of the full submission.

The proportionality calculation of the categories within the entire submission of a given state enabled the research to capture their relative importance and to make comparisons of states' stance regarding the same category. The formula applied for this calculation was:

$$proportion_i = \frac{words_i}{submissions_j}$$

In which:

$$i = 1, \ldots, \ 6 \ (categories \ from \ 1 \ to \ 6)$$

$$j = 1, \ldots, \ 18 \ (submissions \ from \ 1 \ to \ 18)$$

3.3.3 Interpreting Categorical Content Analysis Results in Light of the Oral Statements

The interpretation of the results derived from the categorical analysis was further complemented by an examination of the oral participation of the same states that issued written statements. This helped to identify how the previously defined categories were addressed, emphasised, or reframed in the spoken interventions of state representatives. Of the eighteen states that submitted written statements, fifteen also delivered oral statements, which were analysed in the present book. They are: Bangladesh, Belize, Chile, China, Congo, Djibouti, Guatemala, India, Indonesia, Mauritius, Micronesia, Mozambique, Nauru, Sierra Leone, and Vietnam.

In general, the oral statements reinforced the content of the written submissions, reaffirming core positions and drawing attention to specific legal principles or normative claims already articulated in the documents. This complementary analysis allowed the authors to gain a deeper understanding of the argumentative coherence of each state's position, while also refining the identification of points of convergence and divergence in how different states developed the same topics. Accordingly, the categories that emerged from the analysis of the written submissions—when considered alongside the oral interventions—enabled the authors to trace how Global South states constructed their narratives before the ITLOS advisory proceedings on climate change, highlighting both shared perspectives and distinct approaches.

3.4 An Interdisciplinary Approach: A Qualitative Articulation of Political Context with Legal Argument to Uncover Narratives Advanced Before ITLOS

The final chapter of the book adopts a methodological framework that synthesizes the findings of the previous chapters by using the political context as a lens to identify patterns within the narratives revealed through the legal categories. To achieve this, the authors connected the narratives expressed in state's legal submissions with the political positions articulated in their high-level statements at the UNFCCC COPs. By combining qualitative and quantitative methods, the analysis aimed to uncover similarities and differences in the narratives presented before the ITLOS, shedding light on how legal arguments align with broader political intentions, priorities, and strategies.

3.4.1 Quantitative and Qualitative Examination of Legal Categories

The first step of the '*articulating*' stage involved revisiting the results of the categorical content analysis for each legal category, focusing on the proportion of space different states devoted to each topic within their submissions. This quantification helped identify which states placed the greatest relative emphasis on each category. Within each legal category, the states that stood out in the graphical representations were then grouped according to their level of engagement with the category. To ensure that these findings reflected more than just the amount of textual space allocated, a subsequent qualitative analysis was conducted. This step assessed whether the content of the submissions demonstrated a substantive legal commitment, as opposed to merely rhetorical or superficial references. By combining quantitative prominence with qualitative depth, the study identified which states not only frequently referred to specific legal arguments but also engaged with them in a meaningful manner.

3.4.2 Thematic Grouping of Legal Categories Based on Political Context

The second step examined whether certain legal categories shared underlying thematic similarities, allowing them to be grouped according to broader political context. These thematic clusters were structured in alignment with the political analysis presented in Chap. 4. The first topic examined was the issue of *Inequalities between States*. The analysis aimed to determine whether divergences in legal argumentation were primarily structured along the traditional North–South divide, or whether they revealed internal fractures within the Global South itself. The findings indicated that states prioritizing the legal categories of the *CBDR-RC* principle and *duties of cooperation and assistance* largely framed their arguments within the context of the North–South dichotomy, emphasizing historical responsibility and distributive aspects of climate justice. In contrast, states that focused on the categories of *human rights* and *remedies* articulated a narrative grounded in existential vulnerability, which transcended conventional geopolitical boundaries. This framing highlighted the disproportionate impacts of climate change on certain populations, regardless of their region or level of development. These patterns were further reinforced by the analysis of political discourse at the UNFCCC forums, where the same states echoed similar concerns, aligning their legal reasoning with broader political positions.

A similar analysis was applied to the theme of *Development and Sustainability*. Here, states that emphasized the categories of *CBDR-RC* and *duties of cooperation and assistance* framed climate action as an issue with potential economic consequences, highlighting concerns about its impact on development. On the other hand, states prioritizing the categories of *human rights* and *remedies* framed climate change as an urgent and existential crisis, asserting that economic considerations should not impede global action. This finding was reinforced by the analysis of the stances of the same states in the political arena, in which similar concerns were expressed, mirroring their legal submissions.

The result was translated into two main narratives that represent a division within the Global South, which are *Narratives Uncovering Developmental Interests* (**A**) and *Narratives Uncovering Vulnerabilities* (**B**).

3.4.3 The Role of the Tribunal and States' Views on International Law

The third step involved assessing the legal categories that did not directly correlate with political narratives but instead reflected states' perceptions of the function of ITLOS and international law in addressing climate change. Two key legal categories—*jurisdiction* and *the obligation to prevent pollution of the marine environment*—did not exhibit a clear political correlation but instead revealed states' views on the role of international legal institutions.

States that emphasized *obligation to prevent pollution of the marine environment* appeared to perceive ITLOS as a mechanism to reinforce international environmental commitments, while the rejection of ITLOS *jurisdiction* can be seen as a signal of not wanting international adjudication to deal with the climate matter. Through this analysis, it was found that states emphasizing each of these legal categories correlated with the two dominant narratives of step 2. States prioritising *CBDR-RC* and *cooperation duties* tended to deny jurisdictional authority and, conversely, states emphasizing *human rights* and *state responsibility* were more likely to articulate a stronger reliance on ICTs, demanding a judicial response.

By systematically applying these methodological steps, the book uncovers distinct patterns in how Global South states construct their legal narratives on climate change. Through the identification of alignments and divergences between legal arguments and political positions, the analysis reveals how these narratives reflect emerging internal divisions within the Global South—particularly in relation to development priorities, degrees of vulnerability, and the perceived role of legal institutions in global climate governance.

References

About the secretariat (UNFCCC) https://unfccc.int/about-us/about-the-secretariat. Accessed 16 Oct 2024

Belize (2021) BELIZE—COP 26, CMP 16, CMA 3 First part of the high-level segment. UNFCCC. Available at https://unfccc.int/documents/308162

Benzing (2006) Community interests in the procedure of international courts and tribunals. Law Pract Int Courts Tribun 5

Berlin climate change conference—March 1995 (UNFCCC) https://unfccc.int/conference/berlin-climate-change-conference-march-1995#documents. Accessed 16 Oct 2024

Brazil (2023) Speech by president Lula at the first session of the high-level segment for heads of state and government of COP 28, Presidência Da República. Available at https://www.gov.br/planalto/en/follow-the-government/speeches-statements/2023/speech-by-president-lula-at-the-first-session-of-the-high-level-segment-for-heads-of-state-and-government-of-cop-28

Cardoso Sampaio R, Lyciarão D (2021) Análise de Conteúdo Categorial: manual de Aplicação (Enap)

China (2021) Written statement by Xi HE Jinping, president of people's republic of China at the world leaders summit. UNFCCC. Available at https://unfccc.int/sites/default/files/resource/CHINA_cop26cmp16cma3_HLS-WLS-cn.pdf

China (2022) Continuation of national statements—Message from his excellency Mr. Xie Zhenhua, President Xi Jinping's special representative, China's special envoy for climate change. UNFCCC. Available at https://unfccc-events.azureedge.net/COP27_87675/agenda

China (2023) COP28 summit 2023 LIVE: second part of the high level summit kicks Off at COP28. Youtube. Available at https://www.youtube.com/watch?v=6epub1n2B-Q

Djibouti (2021) Djibouti—High-level segment statement COP 26. UNFCCC. Available at https://unfccc.int/documents/310817

Egypt (2022) President El-Sisi's speech at the opening session of COP 27, state information service. Available at https://www.sis.gov.eg/Story/172566/President-El-Sisi's-Speech-at-the-Opening-Session-of-COP-27?lang=en-us

Egypt (2023) President El-Sisi's speech at UN climate change conference COP28. State information service. Available at https://www.sis.gov.eg/Story/190337/President-El-Sisi

Gang H (2022) The application of narrative research in international relations. In: Proceedings of the 2022 3rd international conference on language, art and cultural exchange, Atlantis Press, 258–261

Gehring T, Spielmann A (2023) The treaty management organization established under the UNFCCC and the Paris agreement: an international actor in its own right? Int Environ Agreements: Polit Law Econ 23:235

Guatemala (2021) Guatemala—High-level segment statement COP 26. UNFCCC. Available at https://unfccc.int/documents/310823

Indonesia (2023) Remarks of president of the republic of Indonesia at the COP28 presidency session at Al Waha theatre, expo city Dubai, Dubai, the United Arab Emirates, Cabinet Secretariat of the Republic of Indonesia. Available at https://setkab.go.id/en/remarks-of-president-of-the-republic-of-indonesia-at-the-cop28-presidency-session-at-al-waha-theatre-expo-city-dubai-dubai-the-united-arab-emirates-december-2-2023/

Kaya Schofield (2020) Which countries send more delegates to climate change conferences? Analysis of UNFCCC COPs 1995–2015. Foreign Policy Anal 16:478

Mayring P (2020) Qualitative content analysis: demarcation, varieties, developments. Forum Qualitative Sozialforschung / Forum: Qualitative Social Research Art 20(3) 16. http://dx.doi.org/10.17169/fqs-20.3.3343

McEnery T, Xiao R, Tono Y (2006) Corpus-based language studies: an advanced resource book. It is designed to represent a specific language or variety of languages, Taylor & Francis

Miskimmon A, O'Loughlin B, Roselle L (2012) Forging the World: Strategic Narratives and International Relations, Royal Holloway

Nauru (2021) Nauru—High-Level segment statement COP 26. Available at https://unfccc.int/documents/476944

Nauru (2022) Resumed high level segment - His excellency Mr. Rennier Stanislaus Gadabu, minister of climate change and national resilience of Nauru. UNFCCC. Available at https://unfccc-events.azureedge.net/COP27_90500/agenda

Nauru (2023) COP28 Summit 2023 LIVE: second Part of the high level summit kicks Off at COP28. Youtube. Available at https://www.youtube.com/watch?v=6epub1n2B-Q

Request for an advisory opinion submitted by the commission of small island states on climate change and international law (request for advisory opinion submitted to the tribunal). https://www.itlos.org/en/main/cases/list-of-cases/request-for-an-advisory-opinion-submitted-by-the-commission-of-small-island-states-on-climate-change-and-international-law-request-for-advisory-opinion-submitted-to-the-tribunal/. Accessed 20 Sept 2024

Sierra Leone (2023) COP 28 High-Level segment - Written statement - Sierra Leone. UNFCCC. Available at https://unfccc.int/documents/637246

UNFCCC (2024) Home https://unfccc.int/. Accessed 3 Oct 2024

University of Connecticut What is the UN COP climate change conference? https://sustainability.uconn.edu/what-is-the-un-cop-climate-change-conference/. Accessed 20 Sept 2024

What Is the United nations framework convention on climate change? UNFCCC. Available at https://unfccc.int/process-and-meetings/what-is-the-united-nations-framework-convention-on-climate-change

Chapter 4
Political Context Surrounding Global South States Narratives on Climate Change

Abstract This chapter analyses the political narratives advanced by Global South states at the high-level segments of the COPs 26, 27, and 28, focusing specifically on the eighteen countries that submitted written statements to the ITLOS advisory proceedings on climate change. Drawing from 54 speeches delivered by heads of government and senior representatives at the COPs' high-level statements, the chapter examines how these states framed their climate concerns in relation to development and justice claims. The analysis identifies two overarching themes: (A) Inequalities Between States and (B) Development and Sustainability. Under the first theme, countries highlighted historical injustices, the North–South divide, and the unequal burden of climate action, often invoking principles like Common But Differentiated Responsibilities. Under the second, they addressed the dual challenge of fostering economic growth while promoting sustainable development, adaptation, and resilience. By tracing how countries articulate vulnerability, solidarity, and differentiated responsibility in political arenas, the chapter offers critical insight into how these discourses inform and resonate with their legal positions in international climate litigation.

Keywords Global South · Climate change · High-level statements · COPs

This chapter examines the participation at the COPs of the Global South states that submitted written statements to the ITLOS advisory proceedings on climate change. The objective is to dissect the political context that underpins the narratives these states presented to the Tribunal. The analysis included 54 statements performed by 18 states at the high-level segments of the COPs 26 (Glasgow, 2021), 27

Lívia Rosas Lamour, researcher at FGV Rio Law's Jean Monnet Centre of Excellence on EU-LA Global Challenges, co-funded by the European Commission, and the Centre for Global Law, is a contributing author to this chapter.

P. Wojcikiewicz Almeida et al., *Uncovering Global South Narratives in ITLOS Advisory Proceedings on Climate Change*, SpringerBriefs in Law,
https://doi.org/10.1007/978-3-032-08427-9_4

(Sharm-el-Sheikh, 2022) and 28 (Abu Dhabi, 2023).[1] The discourses assessed comprised only those delivered at the high-level segments, which represents the most relevant platform in which heads of government and other senior representatives advance their countries' positions on climate change. The discourses presented at the high-level segments were categorised into two main themes: Inequalities Between States (4.1); and Development and Sustainability (4.2).

4.1 Inequalities Between States

While addressing issues of inequality in their high-level statements, several states explicitly evoke the North-South dichotomy to highlight the disparity between developed and developing nations. This framing emphasises how the developed countries of the Global North have historically exploited their natural resources to achieve economic growth, whereas the developing nations of the Global South, while still possessing valuable natural resources, are now being called upon to preserve them in the face of the climate crisis. This discourse underscores the unequal burden placed on the Global South, which is expected to forgo the same resource-intensive development path that the North once followed. Direct references to the Global South were made in the speeches of various states, including China at COP 27[2]; and Brazil,[3] Indonesia,[4] and Sierra Leone[5] at COP 28, reflecting a broader call for climate justice and the recognition of historical responsibilities.

Inequality was also expressed when Global South states emphasised the urgent need for cooperation to achieve development and to create climate-resilient systems. China during COPs 26[6] and 27[7] explicitly referred to multilateralism and collaboration with the G77 countries. While there is broad agreement on the need for financial support from developed nations, the statements reveal differing views on how this assistance should be provided. For instance, countries such as Belize (COP 26)[8] and Djibouti (COP 26)[9] call for direct financial aid from developed countries to mitigate damage or boost resilience to extreme weather

[1] The choice of these fora to assess the political position of the Global South states participating in the ITLOS advisory opinion on climate change was duly justified in the above section concerning the methodology.

[2] China (2022).

[3] Brazil (2023).

[4] Indonesia (2023).

[5] Sierra Leone (2023).

[6] China (2021).

[7] China (2022).

[8] Belize (2021).

[9] Djibouti (2021).

events. Simultaneously, some states have criticised financial barriers imposed by developed nations on the Global South. This criticism was voiced by Sierra Leone (COP 28)[10] and Indonesia (COP 28).[11]

The level of criticism towards the North's lack of cooperation with the South varied throughout the speeches of certain countries. A noticeable shift in tone is particularly evident in the statements delivered by Nauru. The country presented a more moderate stance at COP 26,[12] focusing on a just transition and shared responsibility among states. However, at COP 27,[13] its discourse shifted towards a direct critique of the West, accusing developed nations of failing to fulfil promises on technology transfer, financing, and damage mitigation. At COP 28,[14] this critical tone had softened, with Nauru prioritising calls for financing and support for its partner states, while still maintaining some elements of earlier critique.

Inequalities between States were highlighted not only in the call for cooperation and financial support but also in the advocacy for a climate approach centred on 'Common But Differentiated Responsibilities'. Several countries, including Guatemala (COP 26),[15] Egypt (COPs 27[16] and 28[17]), China (COP 28)[18] and Brazil (COP 28)[19] have directly referenced this principle as a key element of international law. In their direct references to the principle, Global South states also aimed to clarify its practical application within international climate agreements. Djibouti, at COP 28,[20] for instance, argued that the principle should be legally binding for all state members of the UNFCCC, emphasising the need for enforceable commitments. Brazil (COP 28),[21] in turn, underscored the principle's critical importance, stating that it is non-negotiable and must be fully respected in climate negotiations.

Indirect references to the principle of Common but Differentiated Responsibilities (CBDR) are present throughout various speeches. For instance, at COP 26,[22] Egypt called for the recognition of special treatment for African states and argued that Africa is facing its most severe economic, social, political, and security impacts due to climate change. Similarly, other African countries have also used their regional condition to frame climate change concerns. At the same

[10] Sierra Leone (2023).
[11] Indonesia (2023).
[12] Nauru (2021).
[13] Nauru (2022).
[14] Nauru (2023).
[15] Guatemala (2021).
[16] Egypt (2022).
[17] Egypt (2023).
[18] China (2023).
[19] Brazil (2023).
[20] Djibouti (2023).
[21] Brazil (2023).
[22] Egypt (2021).

COP, Sierra Leone[23] and Congo[24] positioned themselves as African states to highlight the continent's vulnerability to desertification, food insecurity, and resource scarcity. Djibouti echoed similar concerns at COP 27,[25] underscoring the shared climate struggles of African nations. These countries present themselves as part of a broader African group directly impacted by global climate dynamics. This collective framing strengthens their calls for support, resilience building, and global climate justice.

Membership to a vulnerable group with shared collective concerns is also evident in Belize's approach at COPs 26,[26] 27,[27] and 28.[28] In its statements, Belize consistently highlighted its status as a Small Island Developing State (SIDS) and member of the Alliance of Small Island States (AOSIS), emphasising that this position makes it particularly vulnerable to climate change. Belize framed its vulnerability as a consequence of its geographical and economic characteristics, which are typical of small island states. This type of framing was also emphasised by other states, such as Nauru[29] and Mauritius[30] at COP 26, and Micronesia at COPs 27[31] and 28.[32] By emphasizing their status as island states, these nations highlighted their vulnerability to climate change, which deeply influences their engagement in the climate debate.

Beyond collective framing, many countries have also highlighted the direct and specific impacts of climate change on their territories. For example, at COP 26, Guatemala,[33] Djibouti,[34] Rwanda,[35] Vietnam,[36] and Mozambique[37] all detailed the various ways in which climate change is causing harm to their countries, such as extreme weather events, loss of biodiversity, and rising sea levels. This pattern was also observed at COP 27, where Brazil,[38] Congo,[39] Chile,[40] and Mauritius[41] outlined

[23] Sierra Leone (2021).
[24] Congo (2021).
[25] Djibouti (2022).
[26] Belize (2021).
[27] Belize (2022).
[28] Belize (2023).
[29] Nauru (2021).
[30] Mauritius (2021).
[31] Micronesia (2022).
[32] Micronesia (2023).
[33] Guatemala (2021).
[34] Djibouti (2021).
[35] Rwanda (2021).
[36] Vietnam (2021).
[37] Mozambique, Discurso Da S. Exa (2021).
[38] Brazil (2022).
[39] Congo (2022).
[40] Chile (2022).
[41] Mauritius (2022).

similar challenges, each offering examples of substantial impact on their environments and economies. At COP 28, Indonesia,[42] Belize,[43] and Guatemala[44] emphasized the unique impacts of climate change on their territories, illustrating the diverse and far-reaching consequences of the global crisis. Due to the referred consequences, these countries requested stronger international support, both in terms of funding and technology transfer, to mitigate the damages and adapt to the climate crisis.

In addressing the national and global perils posed by climate change, some states went even further, framing the environmental crisis as a security issue. Nauru, at COP 27,[45] explicitly described climate change as a critical national security threat, citing existential dangers like rising sea levels and extreme weather events that jeopardise its survival as a nation. Micronesia also invoked security concerns at COPs 27[46] and 28.[47] Several states also addressed the global implications of climate change, such as Guatemala[48] at COP 27 and Brazil[49] at COP 28, in which it reiterated the need for international cooperation to mitigate the global risks posed by climate change. Micronesia,[50] at COP 27, similarly stated that the risks are not confined to low-lying islands. This broader framing highlights the interconnectedness of climate challenges, reinforcing the idea that, for many countries, addressing the environmental crisis is not only a matter of national survival but a global responsibility.

The analysis of the high-level segments concerning the topic *Inequalities Between States* revealed that the discourse of Global South states at the COPs 26, 27 and 28 shared a common storyline, in which these countries emphasized their vulnerability in comparison to the Global North. They also highlighted the need for enhanced cooperation, financial support, and technology transfer. Despite this common framing, African and small island states underscored their heightened vulnerability, attributing it to specific economic and geographic conditions. African states frequently emphasised their continent-wide struggles with desertification, food insecurity, and resource scarcity, while nations like Belize and Mauritius stressed threats from rising sea levels and extreme weather. Countries like Nauru and Micronesia went even further and framed climate change as a security issue, drawing parallels to global conflicts and existential dangers. This nuanced divergence within roughly shared stances reveals the diverse yet interconnected experiences of Global South states in the face of climate change, amplifying their urgent call for justice and meaningful global action.

---

[42] Indonesia (2023).

[43] Belize (2023).

[44] Guatemala (2023).

[45] Nauru (2022).

[46] Micronesia (2022).

[47] Micronesia (2023).

[48] Guatemala (2022).

[49] Brazil (2023).

[50] Micronesia (2022).

4.2 Development and Sustainability

Concerning *Development and Sustainability*, the analysis of the high-level statements seeks to understand Global South states' perspectives towards their development goals, considering climate change and the need for sustainable alternatives. The analysed high-level statements focused on the dual challenge these nations face: promoting economic development while simultaneously addressing climate change. Many Global South states used the high-level segments to advocate for their economic development objectives and to highlight the challenges they encounter in promoting energy transition, climate adaptation, and resilient infrastructure. This reflects their efforts to align national priorities with the global agenda for a sustainable society.

Sustainable development was frequently invoked as a solution in order to balance economic growth and sustainability.[51] At COP 26,[52] Brazil, for instance, recognized both the need for nature protection and the existence of poverty, stating that its actions towards sustainable development could financially benefit those who take care of the forests. Although not directly mentioning sustainable development, China,[53] at COP 26 criticised the model of 'irrational development', aligning its discourse with an approach that seeks to balance ecological sustainability and economic growth. Likewise, China at COP 28[54] stressed that climate action must be combined with the broader framework of achieving sustainable development and eradicating poverty. Nauru[55] at COP 26, on the other hand, discussed how sustainable development should be understood to achieve a 'just transition', meaning a future without fossil fuel dependency. In other cases, whereas still framed as a solution, sustainable development was linked to Sustainable Development Goals (SDGs),[56] as seen in Chile's discourse at COP 26,[57] Sierra Leone's at COP 26,[58] and Mauritius' at COP 27.[59]

In addressing development within the environmental context, some states also expressed the need to address the damages caused by climate change. At COP 26, representatives from Egypt[60] considered adaptation and mitigation efforts as means for the world to 'move forward on equal footing'. The connection between

[51] Ahmad (2020).

[52] Brazil (2021).

[53] China (2021).

[54] China (2023).

[55] Nauru (2021).

[56] IPCC, *Global Warming of 1.5°C: IPCC Special Report on Impacts of Global Warming of 1.5°C above Pre-Industrial Levels in Context of Strengthening Response to Climate Change, Sustainable Development, and Efforts to Eradicate Poverty* (1st ed., IPCC, 2022).

[57] Chile (2021).

[58] Sierra Leone (2021).

[59] Mauritius (2022).

[60] Egypt (2021).

mitigation and adaptation actions with the promotion of a more equal reality was also made at COP 27, where Mozambique[61] emphasised its importance in safeguarding vulnerable communities, ecosystems, and infrastructure from the effects of the environmental crisis. In the same sense, at COP 28, Rwanda[62] criticised the world financial model in which poor countries have to promote mitigation actions through indebtedness. Bangladesh[63] at COP 27 emphasised as a priority limiting temperature rise, securing climate financing, and promoting ‘nature-based climate solutions’. At COP 26, Mozambique,[64] Guatemala,[65] Rwanda,[66] and Mauritius[67] outlined their strategies for addressing climate damage, stressing the innovative character of the initiatives adopted by them. Micronesia[68] and Djibouti[69] also engaged with this critical topic at COP 28, contributing to a broader understanding of the strategies needed to combat climate change effectively. The urgency of sustainable development, mitigation and adaptation actions were frequently associated with concerns about the rights of future and past generations. This was invoked by India[70] and Brazil[71] at COP 26; Congo,[72] Bangladesh,[73] and Mozambique[74] at COP 27; as well as Egypt,[75] Congo,[76] Bangladesh,[77] and Micronesia[78] at COP 28.

Regarding *Development and Sustainability*, the speeches delivered at the COPs 26, 27 and 28 by Global South states revealed a notable emphasis on their developmental needs alongside the commitment to build a sustainable society. This dual focus underscores the urgency of advancing climate efforts, which

---

[61] Mozambique (2022).

[62] Rwanda (2023).

[63] Bangladesh (2022).

[64] Mozambique (2021).

[65] Guatemala (2021).

[66] Rwanda (2021).

[67] Mauritius (2021).

[68] Micronesia (2023).

[69] Djibouti (2023).

[70] India, *National Statement by Prime Minister Shri Narendra Modi at COP26 Summit in Glasgow*, 2021, Ministry of External Affairs Governament of India, available at https://www.mea.gov.in/Speeches-Statements.htm?dtl/34466/National+Statement+by+Prime+Minister+Shri+Narendra+Modi+at+COP26+Summit+in+Glasgow.

[71] Brazil, *supra* note 107.

[72] Congo, *Democratic Republic of Congo—High-Level Segment Statement COP 26*, 2021. UNFCCC, available at https://unfccc.int/documents/310446.

[73] Bangladesh, *supra* note 118.

[74] Mozambique, *supra* note 116.

[75] Egypt, *supra* note 71.

[76] Congo, *COP 28 High-Level Segment—National Statement—Congo*, 2023. UNFCCC, available at https://unfccc.int/documents/635869.

[77] Bangladesh, *COP28 Summit 2023 LIVE: Second Part of the High Level Summit Kicks off at COP28*, 2023. Youtube, available at https://www.youtube.com/watch?v = 6epub1n2B-Q.

[78] Micronesia, *supra* note 86.

were more prominently addressed by African nations and other countries with relatively lower levels of development. The differences in emphasis between the high-level statements reveal a nuanced dynamic within the Global South: while more developed nations often focus on sustainable development as a means to achieve economic growth, countries with lower relative development placed stronger and more urgent emphasis on addressing the damages caused by climate change. Their discourses underpin their disproportionate vulnerabilities and the pressing need for immediate climate action. This nuanced approach in political discourses may also find an echo in the legal arguments addressed by Global South states before the ITLOS advisory proceedings on climate change.

References

Ahmad N (2020) Global south shapers of norms, human development and sustainability. Background Paper, No. 8–2020

Bangladesh (2023) COP28 Summit 2023 LIVE: second part of the high level summit kicks off at COP28. Youtube. Available at https://www.youtube.com/watch?v=6epub1n2B-Q

Bangladesh (2022) Resumed high level segment. UNFCCC. Available at https://unfccc-events.azureedge.net/COP27_90502/agenda

Belize (2021) BELIZE—COP 26, CMP 16, CMA 3 first part of the high-level segment. UNFCCC. Available at https://unfccc.int/documents/308162

Belize (2022) Belize—high-level segment statement COP 27. UNFCCC. Available at https://unfccc.int/documents/623830

Belize (2023) COP 28 high-level segment—national statement—belize. Available at https://unfccc.int/documents/636564

Brazil (2021) Resultados Da COP-26 GovBR. Available at https://www.gov.br/mre/pt-br/canais_atendimento/imprensa/notas-a-imprensa/resultados-da-cop-26

Brazil (2022) Somos Parte Da Solução, Diz Ministro Em Discurso Na Conferência Do Clima. GovBR. Available at https://www.gov.br/mma/pt-br/assuntos/noticias/somos-parte-da-solucao-diz-ministro-em-discurso-na-conferencia-do-clima

Brazil (2023) Speech by President Lula at the first session of the high-level segment for heads of State and Government of COP 28, Presidência Da República. Available at https://www.gov.br/planalto/en/follow-the-government/speeches-statements/2023/speech-by-president-lula-at-the-first-session-of-the-high-level-segment-for-heads-of-state-and-government-of-cop-28

Chile (2021) Chile—high-level segment statement COP 26. UNFCCC. Available at https://unfccc.int/documents/310813

Chile (2022) Resumed high level segment. UNFCCC. Available at https://unfccc-events.azureedge.net/COP27_90502/agenda

China (2023) COP28 Summit 2023 LIVE: second part of the high level summit kicks off at COP28. Youtube. Available at https://www.youtube.com/watch?v=6epub1n2B-Q

China (2021) Written statement by H.E Xi Jinping, President of people's republic of China at the world leaders summit. UNFCCC. Available at https://unfccc.int/sites/default/files/resource/CHINA_cop26cmp16cma3_HLS-WLS-cn.pdf

China (2022) Continuation of national statements—message from his excellency Mr. Xie Zhenhua, President Xi Jinping's Special Representative, China's Special Envoy for Climate Change. UNFCCC. Available at https://unfccc-events.azureedge.net/COP27_87675/agenda

Congo (2021) Democratic Republic of Congo—high-level segment statement COP 26. UNFCCC. Available at https://unfccc.int/documents/310446

Congo (2022) Continuation of national statements. Available at https://unfccc-events.azureedge.net/COP27_87675/agenda
Congo (2023) COP 28 high-level segment—national statement—Congo. UNFCCC. Available at https://unfccc.int/documents/635869
Djibouti (2021) Djibouti—high-level segment statement COP 26. UNFCCC. Available at https://unfccc.int/documents/310817
Djibouti (2022) Resumed high level segment. UNFCCC. Available at https://unfccc-events.azureedge.net/COP27_87675/agenda
Djibouti (2023) COP 28 high-level segment—National Statement—Djibouti. UNFCCC. Available at https://unfccc.int/documents/636242
Egypt (2021) Egypt—high-level segment statement COP 26. UNFCCC. Available at https://unfccc.int/documents/308164
Egypt (2022) President El-Sisi's speech at the opening session of COP 27. State Information Service. Available at https://www.sis.gov.eg/Story/172566/President-El-Sisi's-Speech-at-the-Opening-Session-of-COP-27?lang=en-us
Egypt (2023) President El-Sisi's speech at UN Climate Change Conference COP28. State Information Service. Available at https://www.sis.gov.eg/Story/190337/President-El-Sisi
Guatemala (2021) Guatemala—high-level segment statement COP 26. UNFCCC. Available at https://unfccc.int/documents/310823
Guatemala (2022) Resumed high level segment. UNFCCC. Available at https://unfccc-events.azureedge.net/
Guatemala (2023) COP 28 high-level segment—national statement—Guatemala. UNFCCC. Available at https://unfccc.int/documents/636579
India (2021) National statement by Prime Minister Shri Narendra Modi at COP26 summit in Glasgow. Ministry of External Affairs Governament of India. Available at https://www.mea.gov.in/Speeches-Statements.htm?dtl/34466/National+Statement+by+Prime+Minister+Shri+Narendra+Modi+at+COP26+Summit+in+Glasgow
Indonesia (2023) Remarks of President of the Republic of Indonesia at the COP28 Presidency Session at Al Waha Theatre, Expo City Dubai, Dubai, the United Arab Emirates, December 2, 2023, Cabinet Secretariat of the Republic of Indonesia. Available at https://setkab.go.id/en/remarks-of-president-of-the-republic-of-indonesia-at-the-cop28-presidency-session-at-al-waha-theatre-expo-city-dubai-dubai-the-united-arab-emirates-december-2-2023/
IPCC (2022) Global Warming of 1.5°C: IPCC special report on impacts of global warming of 1.5°C above Pre-Industrial Levels in context of strengthening response to climate change, sustainable development, and efforts to eradicate *Poverty*, 1st edn
Mauritius (2021) Mauritius—high-level segment statement COP 26. UNFCCC. Available at https://unfccc.int/documents/309320
Mauritius (2022) Resumed high level segment. UNFCCC. Available at https://unfccc-events.azureedge.net/COP27_90502/agenda
Micronesia (2022) Federated States of Micronesia—high-level segment statement COP 27. UNFCCC. Available at https://unfccc.int/documents/623866
Micronesia (2023) COP 28 high-level segment—national statement—Micronesia (Federated States Of). UNFCCC. Available at https://unfccc.int/documents/636625
Mozambique (2021) Discurso Da S.Exa Primeiro-Ministro de Moçambique Na Abertura Da COP26. Nações Unidas Moçambique. Available at https://mozambique.un.org/pt/157254-discurso-da-sexa-primeiro-ministro-de-mo%C3%A7ambique-na-abertura-da-cop26
Mozambique (2022) Mozambique—High-level segment statement COP 27. UNFCCC. Available at https://unfccc.int/documents/622779
Nauru (2021) Nauru—high-level segment statement COP 26. Available at https://unfccc.int/documents/476944
Nauru (2022) Resumed high level segment—his Excellency Mr. Rennier Stanislaus Gadabu, Minister of Climate change and national resilience of Nauru. UNFCCC. Available at https://unfccc-events.azureedge.net/COP27_90500/agenda

Nauru (2023) COP28 Summit 2023 LIVE: second part of the high level summit kicks off at COP28. Youtube. Available at https://www.youtube.com/watch?v=6epub1n2B-Q

Rwanda (2021) Rwanda—high-level segment statement COP 26. UNFCCC. Available at https://unfccc.int/documents/309212

Rwanda (2023) National statement at COP28 delivered by Dr Jeanne D'arc Mujawamariya, Minister of Environment. Ministry of Environment. Available at https://www.environment.gov.rw/news-detail/cop-28-national-statement

Sierra Leone (2021) Sierra Leone's President Julius Maada Bio - COP26 Leaders' event: Africa adaptation summit. Global Center on Adaptation. Available at https://gca.org/video/cop26-leaders-event-africa-adaptation-acceleration-summit-h-e-julius-maada-bio-sierra-leone/

Sierra Leone (2023) COP 28 high-level segment—written statement—Sierra Leone. UNFCCC. Available at https://unfccc.int/documents/637246

Vietnam (2021) Viet Nam—high-level segment statement COP 26. UNFCCC. Available at https://unfccc.int/documents/308938

Chapter 5
Global South Narratives Before the ITLOS Advisory Proceedings on Climate Change

Abstract This chapter investigates how Global South states articulate their positions on climate change within the International Tribunal for the Law of the Sea (ITLOS) advisory proceedings. Analyzing written and oral submissions from 18 Global South states, this section employs categorical content analysis to explore their engagement with six key categories: Jurisdiction, Common But Differentiated Responsibilities and Respective Capabilities (CBDR-RC), Duties of Cooperation and Assistance, Obligation to Prevent Marine Pollution, Human Rights, and Remedies. The findings reveal diverse narrative strategies. While most Global South states endorsed ITLOS's advisory jurisdiction, a few, notably Brazil, China, and India, presented robust counterarguments. The CBDR-RC principle emerged as a central theme, with many states emphasizing its role in interpreting UNCLOS obligations, particularly concerning financial and technological support. Similarly, the duty of cooperation and assistance was frequently invoked, often citing international case law to underscore its legally binding nature. The analysis also delves into states' interpretations of the obligation to prevent marine pollution, highlighting the nuanced connection they draw between climate change impacts and existing UNCLOS duties. By examining these narratives embedded in legal arguments, the chapter illuminates how Global South states leverage international legal proceedings to shape legal discourse and advance equitable solutions to the global climate crisis.

Keywords ITLOS advisory opinion on climate change · Categorical content analysis · Global South · Climate change · Common but differentiated responsibilities and respective capabilities

---

Ana Carolina Vasconcelos, PhD candidate in Sociology and Law and MSc in Constitutional Law at the Universidade Federal Fluminense (UFF), is a contributing author to this chapter.

Pedro Henrique Lavinas Ortman, researcher at FGV Rio Law's Jean Monnet Centre of Excellence on EU-LA Global Challenges, co-funded by the European Commission, and the Centre for Global Law, is a contributing author to this chapter.

P. Wojcikiewicz Almeida et al., *Uncovering Global South Narratives in ITLOS Advisory Proceedings on Climate Change*, SpringerBriefs in Law,
https://doi.org/10.1007/978-3-032-08427-9_5

Participation[1] mechanisms in advisory proceedings provide a valuable platform for actors to articulate their positions and motivate broader international engagement on multiple issues. The ITLOS advisory proceedings on climate change highlight the increasing relevance of the law of the sea in addressing the challenges posed by climate change to the marine environment, prompting many participants to engage with the Tribunal to address these issues.

Being international law '*a discourse for crises that lives off crises*',[2] the ITLOS advisory proceedings represent a forum for states to advance their views on the overarching global climate crisis. As jurists often employ storytelling methods to describe the meaning of the law,[3] the legal arguments presented may portray a particular interest, a consolidated position and even preferences on specific related topics, revealing nuances in their narratives. The participants may use a tribunal to convey a particular story through legal arguments as a form of enhancing argumentation and persuasion, or to assert an interpretation, ultimately framing the legal discourse and shaping the understanding and evolution of legal frameworks.[4] The content of such a story embedded within a legal document may be assessed through the analysis of narratives, which aim to explore how a story is told.[5]

To investigate the stories embedded within the legal arguments, this study focuses on the 18 Global South states that submitted written statements to the Tribunal.[6] By analysing such statements according to the 'categorical content analysis' research technique, coupled with an assessment of their oral participation, this chapter explores how these countries engaged with the identified categories: Jurisdiction (5.1); Principle of Common But Differentiated Responsibilities and Respective Capabilities (CBDR-RC) (5.2); Duties of Cooperation and Assistance (5.3); Obligation to Prevent Pollution of the Marine Environment (5.4); Human Rights (5.5); and Remedies (5.6).

These categories were inductively identified through successive rounds of qualitative reading of the written submissions. In the initial stage, the authors conducted an exploratory reading to detect the most frequently addressed themes, followed by additional rounds to refine and consolidate the categories, locate relevant excerpts, and ensure consistency through collaborative discussions and alignment of interpretative criteria. These criteria are detailed in the following sections. The interpretation of the results of the categorical content analysis was further complemented by an examination of the oral statements delivered during public hearings. This additional step made it possible to assess how the same

[1] The authors would like to thank the researcher Lemos Lemos da Silva Walmrath Reis for his excellent research assistance in this chapter.

[2] d'Aspremont (2021).

[3] Otten (2016).

[4] Ibid.

[5] Ibid.

[6] See figure 3.1.

categories were emphasised, reframed, or expanded in the spoken interventions of state representatives, enriching the understanding of the narratives constructed by Global South states before the Tribunal.[7]

5.1 Jurisdiction

The extent to which an international body can request an advisory opinion from the ITLOS as a full court remains contentious since there is no explicit provision on the matter under the UNCLOS.[8] In the advisory opinion requested by the Sub-Regional Fisheries Commission (SRFC),[9] ITLOS asserted that the legal basis to exercise its advisory jurisdiction is found in Article 21 of the Statute.[10] In this opportunity, the ITLOS clarified some normative elements of the provision '[. . .] all matters specifically provided for in any other agreement which confers jurisdiction on the Tribunal', in which 'all matters' does not solely refer to 'disputes' but encompasses advisory opinions.[11] Also, the Tribunal interpreted Article 138 of the Rules of the Tribunal[12] which outlines the prerequisites that must be met for the exercise of the advisory function.[13]

[7] See Chap. 3 to a detailed explanation of the methodological steps.

[8] Tanaka (n 3) 530. The only references to advisory opinions under the law of the sea are those of the ITLOS Sea-Bed Disputes Chamber in response to a request from the Assembly or Council of the International Seabed Authority, see UNCLOS, Article 159(10), 191; Annex VI, Art 40(2).

[9] International Tribunal for the Law of the Sea, Request for Advisory Opinion submitted by the Sub-Regional Fisheries Commission, Advisory Opinion, 2 April 2015, ITLOS Reports 2015, § 58.

[10] ITLOS Statute, Article 21: 'The jurisdiction of the Tribunal comprises all disputes and all applications submitted to it in accordance with this Convention and all matters specifically provided for in any other agreement which confers jurisdiction on the Tribunal.'

[11] International Tribunal for the Law of the Sea, Request for Advisory Opinion submitted by the Sub-Regional Fisheries Commission, Advisory Opinion, 2 April 2015, ITLOS Reports 2015, p. 21, § 54–57.

[12] ITLOS, Rules of the Tribunal, Article 138. '1. The Tribunal may give an advisory opinion on a legal question if an international agreement related to the purposes of the Convention specifically provides for the submission to the Tribunal of a request for such an opinion. 2. A request for an advisory opinion shall be transmitted to the Tribunal by whatever body is authorized by or in accordance with the agreement to make the request to the Tribunal.'

[13] The prerequisites are as follows: (i) an international agreement related to the purposes of the Convention that specifically provides for the submission to the Tribunal of a request for an advisory opinion, (ii) the transmission of the request to the Tribunal by a body authorised by or in accordance with the agreement mentioned above, and (iii) that an opinion may be given on 'a legal question'. See International Tribunal for the Law of the Sea, Request for Advisory Opinion submitted by the Sub-Regional Fisheries Commission, Advisory Opinion, 2 April 2015, ITLOS Reports 2015, p. 21, § 59–60.

The controversy over the ITLOS advisory jurisdiction also appeared during the proceedings on climate change. Although most Global South states—14 out of 18—endorsed the ITLOS's advisory jurisdiction, three Global South states, namely Brazil, China, and India contested the Tribunal's authority to deliver an advisory opinion (Fig. 5.1).

Through categorical content analysis, the extent to which the Global South states engaged with jurisdiction was further explored. The categorization process included a comprehensive analysis of all sections within the written statements that presented arguments pertaining to, either in support of or in opposition to, the jurisdictional authority of the Tribunal. As a result, Fig. 5.2 demonstrates that Brazil (20%), China (50%), and India (20%) dedicated more space to issues concerning jurisdiction in their written submissions compared to other Global South states, as they objected to the exercise of the ITLOS advisory function. However, the arguments within the submissions regarding jurisdictional issues were not solely focused on proving the tribunal lacked the authority to issue an advisory opinion. Some states, with a special emphasis on Guatemala,[14] presented arguments solely concerning jurisdictional matters—corresponding to 50% of its submission—and abstained from delving into the substantive aspects of the case. By contrast, representing only 1% of its written statement, Egypt[15] abstained from making any comments on the jurisdiction of the Tribunal mentioning that it 'will not address, and is without prejudice to its position on, matters related to the Tribunal's jurisdiction'; Bangladesh[16] was the only country that did not address matters of jurisdiction at all, therefore, it does not appear in Fig. 5.2.

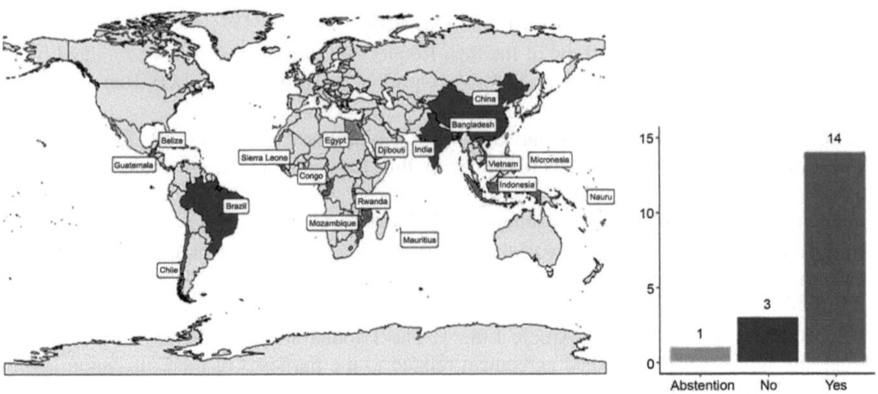

Fig. 5.1 Global South States' positions on matters of jurisdiction: highlighted on world map. *Source* the authors

[14] Written Statement of Guatemala (2023) paras 8–25.

[15] Written Statement of Egypt (2023) para 8.

[16] Written Statement of Bangladesh (2023) para 2.

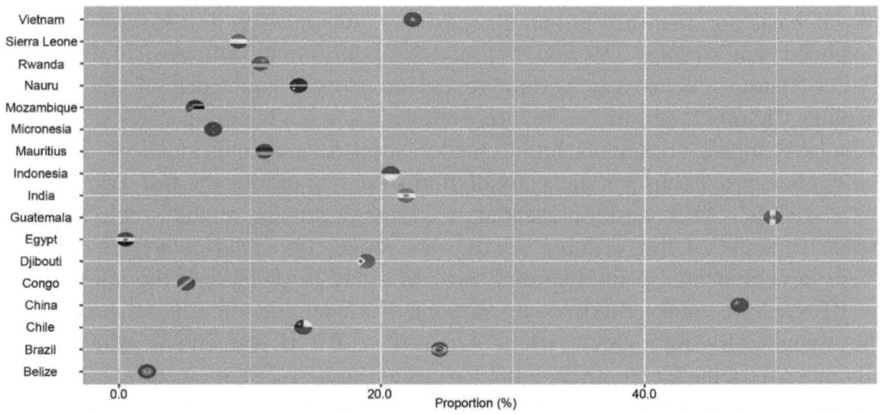

Fig. 5.2 Proportional representation in written statement: Jurisdiction. *Source* the authors

A qualitative analysis of the arguments invoked to deny the jurisdiction of the Tribunal revealed a similar pattern. For instance, Brazil[17] challenged the ITLOS' authority to issue advisory opinions based on the alleged ambiguity of Article 21 of its Statute and contended that the wording 'all matters' allows for 'opposite and equally plausible' interpretations regarding the inclusion of advisory proceedings within its scope. In the absence of clear indication, it argued that one cannot assume that state parties have implicitly conferred such a significant function to the ITLOS. India[18] defended a similar position based on the need for state consent. It argued that the ITLOS Rules of Procedure were intended to govern its internal functioning, and it is not a negotiated text established by an agreement between state parties. It concluded that the inherent powers of a judicial body do not allow the creation of a new jurisdictional authority, which remains paramount for the Tribunal to be able to exercise its powers of interpretation or application of the UNCLOS. China[19] also referred to Article 21 of the ITLOS Statute, contending that the Tribunal cannot establish its advisory jurisdiction solely through implied powers. To support this claim, it posited that the concept of 'implied powers' refers to supplementary powers necessary to bolster the jurisdiction of the Tribunal rather than expanding it. Therefore, China asserted that the Tribunal framed Article 138 of the Rules of the Tribunal for carrying out its functions and cannot grant for itself an advisory jurisdiction exceeding the authorization of UNCLOS and the ITLOS Statute—which do not contain any explicit provision on it.

Oral pleadings revealed additional nuances regarding jurisdiction, notably from China and Micronesia. China, reiterating its opposing stance, contended that neither Article 288 of UNCLOS nor Article 21 of the ITLOS Statute provides

[17] Written Statement of Brazil (2023) paras 5–11.

[18] Written Statement of India (2023) paras 5–8.

[19] Written Statement of China (2023) paras 6–25.

a legal basis for the full Tribunal's advisory competence. Furthermore, China contended that Articles 159 and 191 of UNCLOS, along with Article 40 of the ITLOS Statute, exclusively pertain to the advisory competence of the Seabed Disputes Chamber, and therefore, are irrelevant to the advisory powers of the full Tribunal. China's arguments highlighted a strict textual interpretation, asserting that explicit provisions for such jurisdiction were lacking for the full Tribunal.

In contrast, Micronesia presented a counterargument, emphasizing a more expansive view of the Tribunal's advisory jurisdiction, particularly in light of recent developments in international law. Micronesia pointed to the adoption of the BBNJ Agreement (Biodiversity Beyond National Jurisdiction) in June 2023. They specifically highlighted Article 47(7) of the BBNJ Agreement, which explicitly authorizes the Conference of the Parties to the BBNJ Agreement to request an advisory opinion from the ITLOS. Micronesia emphasized that this article was deliberately negotiated to meet the prerequisites for the full Tribunal's advisory jurisdiction, as previously identified by the Tribunal itself in the SRFC Advisory Opinion. Micronesia further explained that the BBNJ Agreement, being a legally binding instrument negotiated under UNCLOS by all State Parties, holds significant weight. It noted that the President of the ITLOS himself acknowledged this development, stating that "the inclusion of such a provision in the new agreement reflects the potential usefulness of advisory opinions when dealing with complex ocean governance issues".[20] Micronesia concluded that, upon its entry into force, the BBNJ Agreement would represent either subsequent State practice or subsequent agreement of UNCLOS State Parties relevant to the interpretation of UNCLOS, including provisions concerning the Tribunal's advisory jurisdiction. This argument posited that the explicit authorization within the BBNJ Agreement serves as compelling evidence for the full Tribunal's advisory competence.

5.2 Principle of Common but Differentiated Responsibilities and Respective Capabilities

In analyzing the intersection of climate change and the law of the sea, many Global South states stressed the significance of the Common But Differentiated Responsibilities and Respective Capabilities (CBDR-RC) principle, advocating for a more equitable distribution of international obligations. The scope of this principle underscores the duality of a *common* responsibility of all countries to address climate change collaboratively while emphasising the *differentiated* responsibilities tailored to the circumstances of each state.[21] This differentiation recognizes the historical responsibility, the varying national capabilities, and the

[20] Oral Statement of Micronesia (2023) 38.

[21] Ngang (2017).

specific development needs.[22] The CBDR-RC principle provides a legal framework for equitable environmental action by integrating environmental and development concerns and establishing differentiated responsibilities based on individual circumstances.[23] As a central topic in climate negotiations under the UNFCCC and the Paris Agreement, the CBDR-RC has been a significant point of contention, especially surrounding the North-South divide.[24]

The significance of the CBDR-RC principle for Global South states can be assessed by examining whether and how these states articulated their arguments on the topic. To proceed with this investigation, both oral and written statements were categorized to capture the principle's main conceptual elements: This involved identifying explicit references to 'CBDR' or 'CBDR-RC', as well as arguments broadly related to the shared responsibility of states for environmental protection, to the historical contributions to environmental problems, and to the differentiated capacity to address climate change.

The findings demonstrated that most Global South states, notably 13 out of 18, referenced the CBDR-RC principle in their written submissions to support the interpretation of legal obligations under the law of the sea.[25] However, the extent to which these states engaged with this principle CBDR-RC varied significantly. Figure 5.3 illustrates the proportional occurrence with which the CBDR-RC principle was referenced in each Global South written submission. For instance, Brazil was an outlier as it dedicated over 25% of its submission to the topic. Vietnam, Egypt, and India also provided considerable detail on the CBDR-RC principle, dedicating over 10% of their submissions to this topic. However, most Global South states, despite referencing CBDR-RC either directly or indirectly, allocated less than 10% of their written statements to this topic.

The analysis reveals that the 14 Global South countries identified in Fig. 5.3 consistently advocated for the application of the CBDR-RC principle to interpret UNCLOS provisions related to climate change impacts on the marine environment. Brazil, Vietnam, Egypt, and India prominently highlighted the relevance of the CBDR-RC principle in the context of the law of the sea, dedicating substantial portions of their submissions to this topic. Brazil[26] asserted the interpretation of UNCLOS in light of the climate change effects on the oceans 'should be guided by the basic principles of the multilateral climate regime'. It stressed that the CBDR-RC principle strengthens the obligations of states under UNCLOS, especially in the context of financing, capacity building, and technology transfer from developed to

[22] Singh (2022).

[23] P. Sands et al. (2018).

[24] D. Hunter, J. Salzman and D. Zaelke (2022).

[25] Bangladesh, Brazil, Chile, China, Congo, Egypt, India, Mauritius, Mozambique, Nauru, Rwanda, Sierra Leone, Vietnam, and Djibouti.

[26] Written Statement of the Federative Republic of Brazil, *Request For An Advisory Opinion Submitted By The Commission Of Small Island States On Climate Change And International Law*, 2023, International Tribunal for the Law of the Sea, available at https://itlos.org/fileadmin/itlos/documents/cases/31/written_statements/1/C31-WS-1-18-Brazil_01.pdf. at paras 17–19.

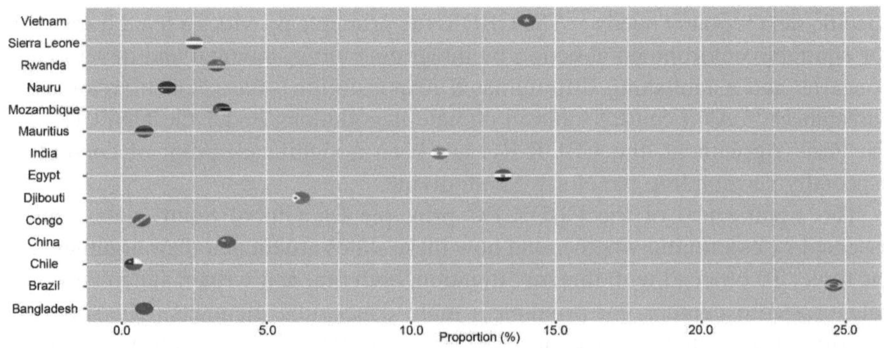

Fig. 5.3 Proportional representation in written statement: Common but Differentiated Responsibilities and Respective Capabilities. *Source* Authors

developing countries. It asserted that this principle is an 'independent source of international law' recognized not only in multilateral climate change agreements, but also in other international treaties, domestic legislation, and decisions of international bodies like the Inter-American Court of Human Rights and the WTO Dispute Settlement Body.

Vietnam[27] argued that the CBDR-RC principle is applicable in the context of UNCLOS concerning the prevention, reduction and control of pollution of the marine environment as a result of climate change. It argued that this generally accepted principle entails specific obligations for states corresponding to their socioeconomic circumstances and historical contributions. In its oral pleading, Vietnam firmly established the CBDR-RC principle as a rule of international law applicable in the relations between the parties to UNCLOS.[28]

India[29] asserted that 'some of the rudiments' of the CBDR-RC principle are set in Part XII of the UNCLOS providing for 'a comprehensive legal framework to protect and preserve the marine environment [. . .] is an essential pillar of the legal order for seas and oceans'. When addressing this topic, it stressed the differentiated responsibilities of developed and developing countries to meet global

[27] Written Statement of the Socialist Republic of Vietnam, *Request For An Advisory Opinion Submitted By The Commission Of Small Island States On Climate Change And International Law*, 2023, International Tribunal for the Law of the Sea, available at https://itlos.org/fileadmin/itlos/documents/cases/31/written_statements/3/C31-WS-3-3-Viet_Nam.pdf. at para 5.1–5.3.

[28] Oral Statement of the Socialist Republic of Vietnam (ITLOS/PV.23/C31/14/Rev.1), *Request For An Advisory Opinion Submitted By The Commission Of Small Island States On Climate Change And International Law*, 2023, International Tribunal for the Law of the Sea, available at https://www.itlos.org/fileadmin/itlos/documents/cases/31/Oral_proceedings/verbatim_records_rev/ITLOS_PV23_C31_14_Rev.1_E.pdf. at p. 45–46.

[29] Written Statement of the Republic of India, *Request For An Advisory Opinion Submitted By The Commission Of Small Island States On Climate Change And International Law*, 2023, International Tribunal for the Law of the Sea, available at https://itlos.org/fileadmin/itlos/documents/cases/31/written_statements/3/C31-WS-3-4-India.pdf. at paras 15–28.

climate goals by referencing the obligations and provisions under the UNFCCC and the Paris Agreement. In addition, it cited the IPCC Reports to argue that between 1850 and 2019, North America and Europe—with a 13% share of the global population—contributed nearly ten times more to global emissions, while South Asia—with about 24% of the global population—accounted for only around 4% of emissions.

Egypt[30] referenced Article 3(1) of the UNFCCC—which underscores the 'principle of equity' and stipulates that developed countries should take the lead in combating climate change due to their historical contributions and greater capabilities—to contend that this framework should guide the implementation of states' obligations under Part XII of UNCLOS. It also highlighted the disproportionate impact of climate change on African countries despite their low GHG emissions to reclaim the need for equitable solutions and support for vulnerable countries.

While some Global South states offered less detailed arguments on the CBDR-RC principle in their submissions, they nonetheless provided valuable insights into its relevance in the context of the law of the sea. Djibouti[31] mentioned that Article 194 of UNCLOS reinforces the CBDR-RC principle by requiring states to use the best available means and act according to their capabilities. Mozambique[32] affirmed that 'there are differential obligations stemming from Part XII of UNCLOS between developed and developing states in relation to the taking of measures to prevent, reduce and control pollution of the marine environment'. Therefore, developed states should bear the primary burden in implementing measures to address marine pollution and in enabling developing countries to meet their responsibilities. Mauritius[33] cited Article 2(2) of the Paris Agreement to emphasize that climate-related duties under Part XII of UNCLOS should be implemented in a manner that reflects equity and the CBDR-RC principle. It suggests that an integrated approach to these duties requires careful consideration of how these principles relate to specific obligations, particularly in light of the support that developed states are obliged to provide to developing ones, especially

[30] Written Statement of the Arab Republic of Egypt, *Request For An Advisory Opinion Submitted By The Commission Of Small Island States On Climate Change And International Law*, 2023, International Tribunal for the Law of the Sea, available at https://itlos.org/fileadmin/itlos/documents/cases/31/written_statements/1/C31-WS-1-17-Egypt.pdf. at para 65.

[31] Written Statement of the Republic of Djibouti, *Request For An Advisory Opinion Submitted By The Commission Of Small Island States On Climate Change And International Law*, 2023, International Tribunal for the Law of the Sea, available at https://itlos.org/fileadmin/itlos/documents/cases/31/written_statements/1/C31-WS-1-31-Djibouti_translation_ITLOS.pdf. at para 57.

[32] Written Statement of the Republic of Mozambique, *Request For An Advisory Opinion Submitted By The Commission Of Small Island States On Climate Change And International Law*, 2023, International Tribunal for the Law of the Sea, available at https://itlos.org/fileadmin/itlos/documents/cases/31/written_statements/1/C31-WS-1-10-Mozambique_01.pdf. at para 3.48.

[33] Written Statement of Mauritius, *Request For An Advisory Opinion Submitted By The Commission Of Small Island States On Climate Change And International Law*, 2023, International Tribunal for the Law of the Sea, available at https://www.itlos.org/fileadmin/itlos/documents/cases/31/written_statements/1/C31-WS-1-12-Mauritius.pdf. at para 70.

those most vulnerable to climate change and with significant capacity constraints. Rwanda[34] identified the CBDR-RC principle as customary international law, reflected in the Rio Declaration, UNFCCC, and Paris Agreement. Similarly, Sierra Leone[35] argued that developed states, following the CBDR-RC principle, must bear the primary burden in addressing climate change. Chile[36] claimed that state parties to the UNCLOS should progressively reduce GHG emissions, reflecting the highest achievable ambition for each state, considering the CBDR-RC, and varying national circumstances.

During the oral pleadings, a point of convergence among several Global South states—Sierra Leone, Bangladesh, Guatemala, Vietnam, China, India, and Congo—was their consistent emphasis on the CBDR principle. Their oral arguments largely mirrored their written submissions, asserting that any interpretation of UNCLOS concerning climate change's negative impacts on the marine environment must be guided by the CBDR principle. These states connected CBDR to the duty to cooperate, particularly regarding technological transfers and financial assistance as outlined in UNCLOS Part XII. While acknowledging that UNCLOS doesn't explicitly mention CBDR, they argued that the principle can nonetheless be inferred from certain provisions, such as Articles 193, 203, and 207. Furthermore, they contended that principles originating from other legal sources, like the international climate change regime, should be systematically interpreted as relevant applicable international law under Article 31(3)(c) of the VCLT.

5.3 Duties of Cooperation and Assistance

Global South states have explored other arguments to promote considerations of equity and fairness regarding their obligations under the UNCLOS. The duty of cooperation and assistance emerged as a key argument governing their obligations under Part XII of UNCLOS. This was referenced in its various forms, including the need for financial assistance, technology transfer, and capacity-building initiatives.

---

[34] Written Statement of the Republic of Rwanda, *Request For An Advisory Opinion Submitted By The Commission Of Small Island States On Climate Change And International Law*, 2023, International Tribunal for the Law of the Sea, available at https://itlos.org/fileadmin/itlos/documents/cases/31/written_statements/3/C31-WS-3-1-Rwanda.pdf. at paras 303 and 290–314.

[35] Written Statement of the Republic of Sierra Leone, *Request For An Advisory Opinion Submitted By The Commission Of Small Island States On Climate Change And International Law*, 2023, International Tribunal for the Law of the Sea, available at https://itlos.org/fileadmin/itlos/documents/cases/31/written_statements/1/C31-WS-1-29-Sierra_Leone.pdf. at para 62.

[36] Written Statement of the Republic of Chile, *Request For An Advisory Opinion Submitted By The Commission Of Small Island States On Climate Change And International Law*, 2023, International Tribunal for the Law of the Sea, available at https://itlos.org/fileadmin/itlos/documents/cases/31/written_statements/1/C31-WS-1-20-Chile_01.pdf. at para 57–58.

Methodologically, the categorization of Global South states' written statements on duties of cooperation and assistance considered both the explicit use of these terms and citations of UNCLOS provisions containing such obligations (Article 197, 198, 202 and 203). This also included references to scientific and technical assistance and the duties of information sharing and notification. A quantitative analysis, based on the proportional representation of duties of cooperation and assistance in written statements, indicated that 13 out of 18 Global South states addressed the topic. As Fig. 5.4 illustrates, China, Brazil and India dedicated proportionally more space in their submissions to issues of cooperation and assistance, followed by Chile and Egypt.

At least seven states, including Brazil,[37] Egypt,[38] Congo,[39] Mozambique,[40] Chile,[41] Rwanda,[42] and Mauritius[43] referred to the ITLOS' case law as far as the duty of cooperation is concerned. The MOX Plant case was mentioned to highlight that '[T]he duty to cooperate is a fundamental principle in the prevention of pollution of the marine environment under Part XII of the Convention and general international law'.[44] Most of these states stressed the importance of international cooperation and mentioned Part XII of UNCLOS, which contains provisions establishing an obligation to cooperate (Articles 197 to 203). Djibouti,[45] Belize[46] and Mozambique[47] echoed this in its oral pleading, drawing on MOX Plant for the practical implications of this duty, such as consultations and joint work on international standards. Djibouti also invoked the International Court of Justice's *Pulp Mills* case,[48] quoting that 'it is by cooperating that the States will can jointly manage the risks of damage to the environment'.[49]

[37] Written Statement of the Federative Republic of Brazil, *supra* note 155, at para 15.

[38] Written Statement of the Arab Republic of Egypt, *supra* note 158, at paras 51–52.

[39] Written Statement of the Democratic Republic of the Congo, *Request For An Advisory Opinion Submitted By The Commission Of Small Island States On Climate Change And International Law*, 2023, International Tribunal for the Law of the Sea, available at https://itlos.org/fileadmin/itlos/documents/cases/31/written_statements/1/C31-WS-1-1-RD_Congo_translation_ITLOS.pdf. at para 215.

[40] Written Statement of the Republic of Mozambique, *supra* note 160, at para 4.20.

[41] Written Statement of the Republic of Chile, *supra* note 164, at para 81.

[42] Written Statement of the Republic of Rwanda, *supra* note 162, at para 196.

[43] Written Statement of Mauritius, *supra* note 161, at para 76.

[44] International Tribunal for the Law of Sea, *MOX Plant (Ireland v. United Kingdom)*, Provisional Measures, Order of 3 December 2001, ITLOS Reports 2001, p. 95., para 82.

[45] Oral Statement of Djibouti, p. 31.

[46] Oral Statement of Belize, p. 40.

[47] Oral Statement of Mozambique, p. 19.

[48] International Court of Justice, *Pulp Mills on the River Uruguay (Argentina v. Uruguay)*,.

[49] Oral Statement of Djibouti, p. 31.

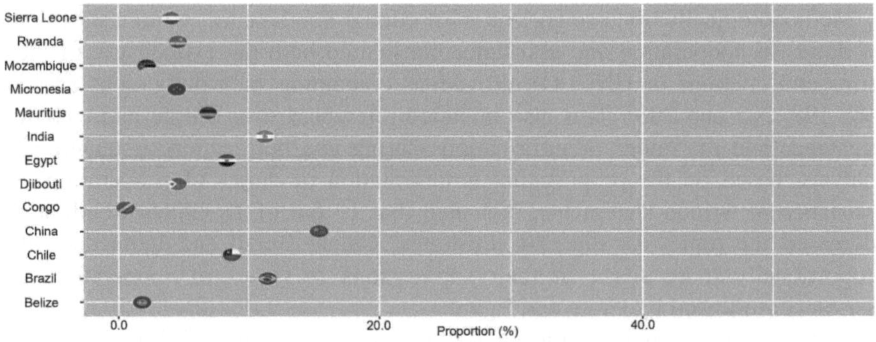

Fig. 5.4 Proportional Representation in Written Statement: Duties of Cooperation and Assistance. *Source* Authors

At least eight states, including Brazil,[50] Egypt,[51] Sierra Leone,[52] Micronesia,[53] Mozambique,[54] Chile,[55] Rwanda,[56] and Mauritius[57] invoked Article 197 of the UNCLOS on the 'cooperation on a global or regional basis', which establishes the obligations of cooperation for the protection and preservation of the marine environment, specifically related to the formulation and elaboration of international rules, standards, and recommended practices and procedures. Egypt,[58] Micronesia[59] and Rwanda[60] also referred to Article 198 of UNCLOS which delineates the obligation of 'notification of imminent or actual damage' of marine pollution. Micronesia argued that this provision 'imposes a duty of immediate notification by a state to other states

[50] Brazil defines it as "general duty of international cooperation for the protection and preservation of the marine environment". See Written Statement of the Federative Republic of Brazil, *supra* note 155. at para 14.

[51] Written Statement of the Arab Republic of Egypt, *supra* note 158., at para 50.

[52] Written Statement of the Republic of Sierra Leone, *supra* note 163., at para 66.

[53] Written Statement of the Federated State of Micronesia, *Request For An Advisory Opinion Submitted By The Commission Of Small Island States On Climate Change And International Law*, 2023, International Tribunal for the Law of the Sea, available at https://itlos.org/fileadmin/itlos/documents/cases/31/written_statements/1/C31-WS-1-30-FS_Micronesia_01.pdf. at para 60.

[54] Mozambique contended that this 'provision establishes a specific but broad obligation for States to cooperate in the protection of the marine environment'. See: Written Statement of the Republic of Mozambique.

[55] Chile affirmed that "the duty to cooperate of article 197 applies to all maritime zones". See: Written Statement of the Republic of Chile, at para 103.

[56] Written Statement of the Republic of Rwanda, at para 306.

[57] Written Statement of Mauritius, at para 76.

[58] Written Statement of the Arab Republic of Egypt, at para 50.

[59] Written Statement of the Federated States of Micronesia, at para 37.

[60] Written Statement of the Republic of Rwanda, at para 198.

when the marine environment 'is in imminent danger of being damaged or has been damaged by pollution'.[61]

Notably, the provisions concerning the duty of assistance of developed to developing countries, in particular Article 202 (on scientific and technical assistance to developing states) and 203 (on preferential treatment for developing states) of the UNCLOS, were extensively referenced by the Global South states. Brazil[62] submitted that 'the Convention recognizes the obligation to grant special treatment to developing states in the allocation of appropriate funds and technical assistance from international organizations and the utilization of their specialized services'. Egypt[63] recalled that Article 203 'provides for the preferential treatment by international organisations for developing states in the allocation of relevant funds and technical assistance'. In Chile's view[64] 'cooperation between states should go hand in hand with coordination'. It complemented that it is due to cooperation mechanisms 'in the form of the allocation of funds, technical assistance and the utilisation of specialised services through international organisations' that developing countries can undertake measures to protect and preserve the marine environment and to adapt to the consequences of climate change.

China[65] highlighted the interconnectedness of financing, technology, and capacity-building while recalling that developed countries need to honour their commitment to providing '$100 billion annually' to developing countries as climate finance. It further added that developed countries should establish a roadmap for doubling adaptation finance and contribute to the Loss and Damage Fund. China dedicated a whole section to expose its initiative to 'vigorously promote international cooperation on climate change'. It stressed how the country has been fostering South-South cooperation by providing support 'for fellow developing countries within its capabilities'.[66]

India[67] referred to other international legal instruments, such as the UNFCCC and the Paris Agreement and called for international cooperation as a means of enabling all states to meet their climate change goals, stressing the importance of technology transfer from developed to developing countries. India further stated that developing countries 'cannot deploy low-carbon climate technologies at a significant scale unless a facilitative global technology transfer regime is in

[61] Written Statement of the Federated States of Micronesia, at para 37.

[62] Written Statement of the Federative Republic of Brazil, at para 5.

[63] Written Statement of the Arab Republic of Egypt, at para 59.

[64] Written Statement of the Republic of Chile, *supra* note 164., at paras 105–111.

[65] Written Statement of the People's Republic of China, *Request For An Advisory Opinion Submitted By The Commission Of Small Island States On Climate Change And International Law*, 2023, International Tribunal for the Law of the Sea, available at https://itlos.org/fileadmin/itlos/documents/cases/31/written_statements/1/C31-WS-1-8-China__transmission_ltr._.pdf. at paras 29 and 36.

[66] See Ibid., at para 36.

[67] Written Statement of the Republic of India, *supra* note 157., at paras 30–31.

place', and the 'incremental and associated costs of these are met by grant-based and concessional public-sources finance provided by developed countries'.[68]

Although the quantitative analysis indicates that the arguments concerning cooperation and assistance were proportionally less expressive in Sierra Leone and Djibouti's written submissions (5% of the document), they outlined the dependence on support provided by developed countries to fulfil their climate-related obligations. Sierra Leone[69] suggested that financial assistance and technological resources to African countries effectively enable these countries to implement their national climate change strategies. It concluded that without this support from developed states, developing countries may be unable to implement effective mitigation measures rendering it difficult to fulfil their obligations under UNCLOS to protect the marine environment from climate change impacts. Similarly, Djibouti[70] reiterated its extreme vulnerability to climate change, being one of the least developed countries to indicate that to achieve its GHG reduction targets it 'would have to invest more than USD 3.8 billion'.

5.4 Obligation to Prevent Pollution of the Marine Environment

The first question of the COSIS request[71] for an advisory opinion submitted to the ITLOS pursues a twofold clarification specifically related to the obligation to prevent pollution of the marine environment. Since the connection between ocean and climate change is not explicit under the law of the sea, this inquiry aims to delineate the 'specific' obligations that derive from the broad obligation to prevent pollution of the marine environment under UNCLOS as a result of the climate change effects.

To investigate how the Global South states explored the intricate connection between marine pollution and climate change and the specific obligations that stem from it, the categorisation encompassed explicit references to the expression 'obligation to prevent pollution of the marine environment' (and its similar spelling, such as 'prevention'). Also, it included the citation and the subsequent arguments on the main provisions of Part XII of the UNCLOS which concern the *specific* obligations to prevent pollution of the marine environment, such as Articles 194 (Section 1, on *General Provisions*); 204, 205, 206 (Section 4, on *Monitoring and Environmental Assessment*); 207, 212 (Section 5, on *International Rules and National Legislation to Prevent Reduce and Control Pollution of the Marine Environment*); 213, and 222 (Section 5, on *Enforcement*). Figure 5.6

[68] Written Statement of the People's Republic of China, *supra* note 190.

[69] Written Statement of the Republic of Sierra Leone, *supra* note 163., at para 62 and 90.

[70] Written Statement of the Republic of Djibouti, *supra* note 159., at para 59.

[71] See Introduction.

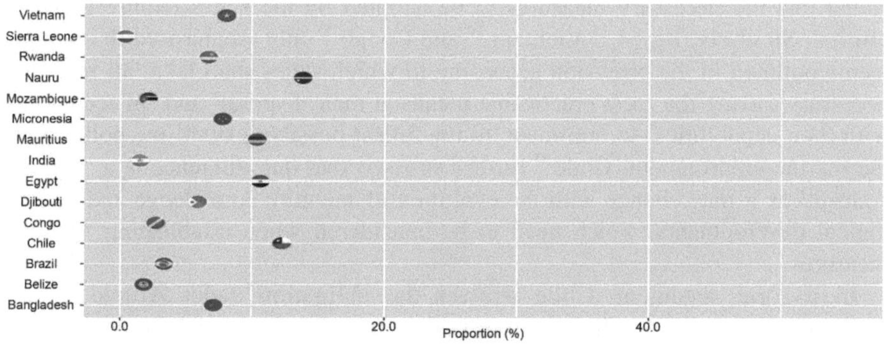

Fig. 5.5 Proportional Representation in written statement: Obligation to Prevent Pollution of the Marine Environment. *Source* Authors

offers a visual representation of the countries that prioritized the broad obligation to prevent marine pollution, demonstrating their emphasis on this issue, both with and without a direct connection to the impacts of climate change. Although this subject was central to the discussion of the request, Chile, Egypt, and Mauritius used around 10% of their written statement to present arguments associated with this topic, whereas it represented less than 5% of Brazil, Belize, Congo, Mozambique, India, and Sierra Leone's statements.

While the quantitative data in Fig. 5.5 may not fully capture the extent of their engagement, a qualitative analysis provides a deeper understanding of how certain countries addressed the subject within their arguments. This was relevant to further observe whether and how the Global South states *(i)* perceived the UNCLOS normative gap concerning the impacts of climate change in connection with existing obligations to prevent marine pollution and *(ii)* identified the specific obligations to support this preventive duty.

Initially, on the *General Provisions* (Part XII, Section 1 of the UNCLOS) the central obligation under Article 194 of UNCLOS on the 'measures to prevent, reduce and control pollution' was referenced by multiple states[72] as an obligation of conduct—a due diligence obligation—and not of result. However, the threshold of the expected measure to be adopted was developed in different degrees by the states. Mauritius[73] and Chile[74] simply cited the provision whereas Brazil[75] only

[72] International Tribunal of the Law of the Sea. Request for an advisory opinion submitted by the Commission of Small Island States on Climate Change and International Law: Written Statement of India (2023) para 12; Written Statement of Egypt (2023) para 38–45; Written Statement of Vietnam (2023) para 4.4; Written Statement of Bangladesh (2023) para 35–42; Written Statement of Congo (2023) paras 192–194; Written Statement of Rwanda (2023) paras 190 and 222; Written Statement of Mauritius (2023) para 82; Written Statement of Nauru (2023) paras 40–45.

[73] Written Statement of Mauritius (2023) para 76.

[74] Written Statement of Chile (2023) para 102–103.

[75] Written Statement of Brazil (2023) para 14.

added that the necessary measures to be adopted by the states require the 'best efforts'. Similarly, Egypt,[76] Vietnam,[77] and Congo[78] only emphasised the requirements outlined in the provision according to which states shall take 'all measures necessary', using the 'best practicable means at their disposal' and 'in accordance with their capabilities' to minimise 'to the fullest possible extent' the pollution of the marine environment. Chile[79] further stressed that due diligence is a 'variable concept' as it may change with the evolution of scientific knowledge and technological developments, which need to be considered when establishing adequate measures.

In its oral statement, Chile stresses the obligation under Article 194 of UNCLOS as one of conduct. It asserts that state Parties to the Convention are required to 'take all measures necessary to prevent, reduce and control pollution of the marine environment [. . .] in relation to climate change impacts'.[80] Chile explicitly links UNCLOS to the UNFCCC and the Paris Agreement, arguing that if the commitments under the Paris Agreement prove insufficient to ensure the protection of the marine environment, UNCLOS remains fully capable of addressing the deleterious effects of climate change on the ocean, by virtue of the obligations enshrined in Article 194. Although with less emphasis than Chile, Vietnam's[81] oral statement similarly highlighted that UNCLOS obligations are applicable to the prevention of pollution resulting from 'anthropogenic greenhouse gas emissions'. In sum, beyond the mere citation of the requirements of Article 194 of the UNCLOS, Chile and Vietnam, in their oral participation, developed a connection between climate change-related obligations with the necessary measures to prevent marine pollution.

Other states also developed such connection in their written submissions. Despite the absence of any reference to climate change under the UNCLOS, Bangladesh[82] for instance stated that Part XII of the Convention 'places specific obligations to GHG emissions that result in deleterious effects related to climate change and to protect and preserve the marine environment from those effects'. Likewise, Belize[83] and

[76] Egypt refers to the reasoning of the ITLOS Seabed Dispute Chamber in *Responsibilities of States in the Area*: 'adequate means, to exercise best possible efforts, to do the utmost, to bring this result'. Written Statement of Egypt (2023) para 45.

[77] Vietnam adds a reference to the *South China Sea Arbitration* delivered by the Permanent Court of Arbitration that ruled that the State has to ensure that activities under their jurisdiction or control do not cause damage to others. Written Statement of Vietnam (2023) para 4.4.

[78] Congo stressed that the 'fullest possible extent' should be understood as not mere effort but on the contrary the greatest conceivable effort. Written Statement of Congo (2023) para 190.

[79] Written Statement of Chile (2023) paras 79–80 and 96.

[80] Oral Statement of Chile (2023) p. 9.

[81] Oral Statement of Vietnam (2023) p. 10.

[82] Written Statement of Bangladesh (2023) para 27.

[83] Belize elaborated that 'in the absence of such regulations, the necessary measures would be assessed by multiple factors, including with reference to (a) Application of the precautionary principle alongside identification and application of the best scientific means available; (b) The

Sierra Leone[84] and Nauru[85] stated that all necessary measures should be employed by the states to limit global average temperature rise to 1.5°C above pre-industrial levels considering the scientific consensus. Rwanda[86] and Mozambique[87] also argued that such measures should be adopted to prevent pollution 'in the form of GHG emissions' from activities under the jurisdiction or control of the states. Similarly, Bangladesh,[88] Belize,[89] Sierra Leone,[90] and Mozambique[91] linked obligations under Article 194 of UNCLOS to climate-related issues also in their oral statements. Bangladesh explicitly stated that state parties to the Convention are committed 'to prevent, reduce and control pollution of the marine environment in relation to the deleterious effects that result or are likely to result from climate change', according to their respective capabilities.

To further delineate the specific obligations some states relied on Articles 207 and 212 of Part XII, Section 5 of the UNCLOS on the *International Rules and National Legislation to Prevent Reduce and Control Pollution of the Marine Environment.* Considering pollution from land-based sources[92] and from or through the atmosphere,[93] both provisions require the state parties to *(i)* at the national level, adopt legislation considering internationally agreed rules, standards and recommended practices and procedures and *(ii)* at the international level, develop global and regional regulation, especially through international organisations or diplomatic conferences. Briefly, Micronesia[94] stressed the importance of the multi-layered system of regulation, including domestic and international spheres. Rwanda[95] drew a connection with climate change by arguing that states need to adopt global rules to specifically mitigate GHG emissions from activities taking place within their

need for measures to be effective; (c) Reports such as those of the Intergovernmental Panel on Climate Change ("IPCC"); (d) Other obligations of the relevant State, including within the framework of the UNFCCC; and (e) As applicable, the results of relevant monitoring and environmental assessment.' Written Statement of Belize (2023) para 89.

[84] Written Statement of Sierra Leone (2023) para 57.

[85] Written Statement of Nauru (2023) paras 46–50.

[86] Written Statement of Rwanda (2023) para 223.

[87] Mozambique argued that the standard of due diligence has to be more severe for riskier activities in light of the precautionary principle, even for activities where the scientific evidence is not as developed or where the deleterious effects are not fully clear the states are obliged to adopt regulations limiting their GHG emissions. Written Statement of Mozambique (2023) paras 3.61–3.77.

[88] Oral Statement of Bangladesh (2023) p. 20.

[89] Oral Statement of Belize (2023) p. 32.

[90] Oral Statement of Sierra Leone (2023) p. 31.

[91] Oral Statement of Mozambique (2023) p. 11–13.

[92] Article 207 UNCLOS.

[93] Article 212 UNCLOS.

[94] Written Statement of Micronesia (2023) paras 60–62.

[95] Written Statement of Rwanda (2023) para 219.

jurisdiction or under their control. Also, Nauru[96] stressed that the provisions of the Paris Agreement shall be considered when referring to internationally agreed rules, standards, and recommended practices and procedures.

Interestingly, only Article 207 of UNCLOS determined that these ‘laws, regulations, measures, rules, standards and recommended practices’ shall take into consideration ‘regional features, the economic capacity of developing states and need for economic development’.[97] On this topic, Chile, Rwanda, and Belize[98] emphasised the importance of considering the developmental differences of each state when undertaking international regulations.

On the *Enforcement* (Section 6 of Part XII of the UNCLOS) of these laws and regulations, Rwanda[99] briefly cited Articles 213 and 222. Micronesia, Egypt, Nauru and Vietnam[100] argued for a more stringent enforcement obligation by arguing that beyond adopting regulations, state parties shall implement a ‘certain level of vigilance’ and exercise ‘administrative control’.

Some states stressed the specific obligations under Articles 204, 205, and 206 of Part XII, Section 4 of the UNCLOS, on *Monitoring and Environmental Assessment*. Regarding the topic, Micronesia,[101] Rwanda,[102] and Mauritius[103] stressed the obligations of *(i)* monitoring the risks or effects of pollution of the marine environment, *(ii)* conducting an assessment of potential effects of planned activities under jurisdiction or control that may cause substantial pollution to the marine environment and may have a significant adverse impact in a transboundary context and *(iii)* communicating these results to competent

[96] Written Statement of Nauru (2023) para 45.

[97] Article 207 (4) and (5) UNCLOS.

[98] Written Statement of Chile (2023) para 49; Written Statement of Egypt (2023) paras 46–49, Written Statement of Belize (2023) paras 84–85, Written Statement of Rwanda (2023) paras 213, 219, 226–231, 238, 274, 302.

[99] Written Statement of Rwanda (2023) paras 233 and 238.

[100] Written Statement of Micronesia (2023) para 62; Written Statement of Egypt (2023) para 49; Written Statement of Vietnam (2023) para 4.4; Written Statement of Nauru (2023) para 40.

[101] Written Statement of Micronesia (2023) para 38.

[102] Rwanda refers to the decision of the Seabed Disputes Chamber in the Advisory Opinion on *Activities in the Area*, to uphold that this obligation to exercise due diligence in preventing significant transboundary harm requires environmental impact assessment to be conducted if there is a risk of significant transboundary harm prior to undertaking an activity reflects a broader requirement of customary international law affirmed by the International Court of Justice in *Pulp Mills on the River Uruguay* (Argentina v. Uruguay), Judgment I.C.J. Reports 2010 (I), p. 73, para. 204; *Certain Activities Carried Out by Nicaragua in the Border Area* (Costa Rica v. Nicaragua) and *Construction of a Road in Costa Rica along the San Juan River* (Nicaragua v. Costa Rica), Judgment, I.C.J. Reports 2015, p. 665; pp. 706–707, para. 104; see also, ibid, at p. 720 para. 153. Written Statement of Rwanda (2023) para 203–204.

[103] The State also refers to *Pulp Mills on the River Uruguay* (Argentina v. Uruguay) to uphold that this is an obligation under general international law. ‘Written Statement of Mauritius’ (2023) paras 81–83.

international organisations. Mauritius[104] was the only state to correlate these obligations with climate change effects, arguing that they must be interpreted in light of the 'UNFCCC/Paris Agreement specific elements of impact assessment relating to projects given rise to GHG emissions', adding that these assessments should include a metric for measuring the impact on ocean acidification. It emphasised that publicity and communication must align with the transparency framework of Article 13 of the Paris Agreement and shall be published under the authority of the UNFCCC and the Paris Agreement. Nauru,[105] despite referencing Article 194 (2) of the UNCLOS, also mentioned the obligation to conduct an environmental impact assessment, specifically relating it with activities likely to cause transboundary harm from greenhouse gas emissions.

5.5 Human Rights

Human rights were not a focus of the negotiations between the state parties to the UNCLOS.[106] As a result, references to human rights in this Convention appear only indirectly, generally associated with increased cooperation in international relations, either by improving the quality of life resulting from the exploitation of ocean resources[107] or by protecting human rights on the high seas.[108] The interconnectedness between the law of the sea and human rights became more relevant when climate change came to be understood as a violation of human rights.[109]

The categorization of Global South states' submissions on the topic of 'human rights' was not investigated through the number of references to the term 'human rights',[110] as it encompasses the entire arguments on the effects of climate change on persons and the vulnerability of communities and areas affected or more prone to climate catastrophes (Fig. 5.6).

Nauru[111] stood out for its emphasis on human rights and the harmful effects of climate change on human life. It argued that climate change poses a significant

---

[104] Written Statement of Mauritius (2023) para 43.

[105] Written Statement of Nauru (2023) para 44.

[106] Billing (2024).

[107] Ibid.

[108] Bastos (2024).

[109] Billing (2024).

[110] A quantitative analysis showed that 10 out of 18 countries expressly mentioned the keyword 'human rights' in their submissions, whereas Congo cited it more than 100 times; and Chile, Micronesia and Nauru used it around 10 times. Nonetheless, the number of citations of the keyword does not necessarily indicate the depth of argumentation concerning human rights.

[111] Written Statement of the Republic of Nauru, *Request For An Advisory Opinion Submitted By The Commission Of Small Island States On Climate Change And International Law*, 2023, International Tribunal for the Law of the Sea, available at https://itlos.org/fileadmin/itlos/documents/cases/31/written_statements/1/C31-WS-1-22-Nauru.pdf. at para 5.

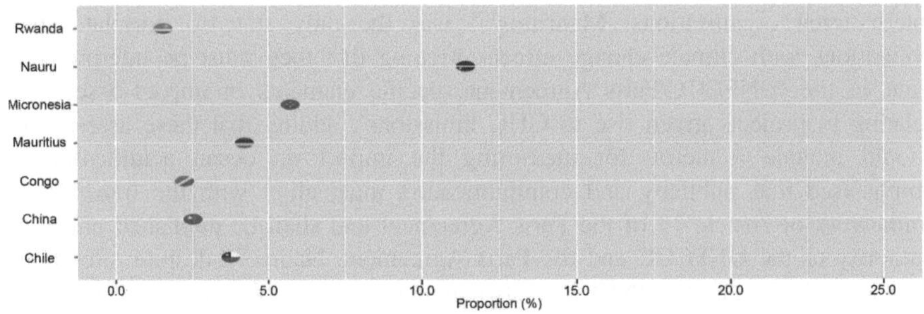

Fig. 5.6 Proportional representation in written statement: Human Rights. *Source* Authors

threat to its population's livelihood, well-being, and means of subsistence. Also, Nauru cited the International Covenant on Civil and Political Rights (ICCPR), the International Covenant on Economic, Social and Cultural Rights (ICESCR) and General Comment N.12 of the Human Rights Committee as interpretative guidance to the UNCLOS. These instruments were mobilised to contend that Article 192 of the UNCLOS should be interpreted as to guarantee that climate change effects on the marine environment do not deprive access to people of their means of subsistence. Similarly, Congo[112] mentioned universal and regional instruments for the protection of human rights related to the interpretation of UNCLOS throughout its submission. It especially highlighted the inequalities caused by climate change, which tends to affect the most vulnerable sectors of societies. Moreover, it claimed access to justice as an important means when confronting the climate crisis.

In addition, the five categorised states in Fig. 5.5 stressed the bond between climate change and human rights, by initially contextualizing the negative impacts of climate change on the environment, economic development and prosperity, and the promotion and protection of human living conditions. These harmful effects were used by these states—Nauru,[113] Congo,[114] Rwanda,[115] Micronesia,[116] Mauritius[117] and Chile[118]—to further argue that the UNCLOS should be interpreted alongside human rights, climate change and environmental protection norms.

Nauru, Congo, Micronesia, Mauritius, Chile and Sierra Leone also took part in oral pleadings and addressed human rights. Micronesia stressed in oral pleadings the consideration for a special attention towards the rights of indigenous peoples in

[112] Written Statement of the Democratic Republic of the Congo, *supra* note 167. at paras 98–105; 113–116.

[113] Written Statement of the Republic of Nauru, *supra* note 200. at paras 71–80.

[114] Written Statement of the Democratic Republic of the Congo, *supra* note 167. at paras 99–104.

[115] Written Statement of the Republic of Rwanda, *supra* note 162. at paras 38–52.

[116] Written Statement of the Federated States of Micronesia, *supra* note 176. at paras 90–94.

[117] Written Statement of Mauritius, *supra* note 161. para 60.

[118] Written Statement of the Republic of Chile, *supra* note 164. at para 69.

relation to UNCLOS. It asserts that indigenous peoples possess collective rights over their traditional territories, including vital coastal and maritime spaces. Harms to these territories from anthropogenic greenhouse gas emissions, Micronesia argues, directly hamper the enjoyment of these rights. Micronesia highlights that the rights of indigenous peoples, whether seen as a subset of broader human rights or a distinct body of international law, are integral to the international rules and standards governing the protection and preservation of the marine environment from human-induced greenhouse gas emissions. This means that UNCLOS States Parties have a clear obligation to engage in intergovernmental and domestic processes to prevent, reduce, and control emissions to the extent required for indigenous peoples to fully exercise their rights, which are deeply dependent on a healthy marine environment. A failure to ensure this healthy environment due to emissions, Micronesia concludes, constitutes a clear breach of States Parties' obligations under UNCLOS. Furthermore, any assessment of climate change's impacts on the marine environment, and the subsequent measures taken, must not only consider the best available science but also fully incorporate the relevant knowledge of indigenous peoples and local communities regarding their traditional marine environments. This underscores a call for an inclusive, rights-based approach to marine environmental protection that recognizes and values indigenous knowledge alongside scientific data.

5.6 Remedies

Holding states responsible for committing illegal acts, violating treaties or transgressing the rules of customary law derives from the necessity to pressure compliance with international obligations.[119] Promoting state responsibility for unlawful acts is a possible way to address environmental challenges, especially those concerning cessation, guarantees of non-repetition, and even compensation for damage.[120] Nevertheless, providing adequate reparations to address excessive GHG emissions poses significant challenges as the damages are widespread and not directed at a particular state.[121]

In conducting our analysis, the categorization process was fundamentally guided by a focus on arguments that directly engaged with international responsibility in its broader sense. This included, but was not limited to, the explicit invocation of the strict concept of "state responsibility", as well as its conceptual synonyms and derivatives. This included scrutinizing the express use of terms such as 'remedies', 'liabilities', and 'reparation'—encompassing 'restitution', 'compensation', and 'damages'. Furthermore, the analysis extended to instances where the

[119] B. Mayer (2018).

[120] Voigt (2021).

[121] Mayer (2018).

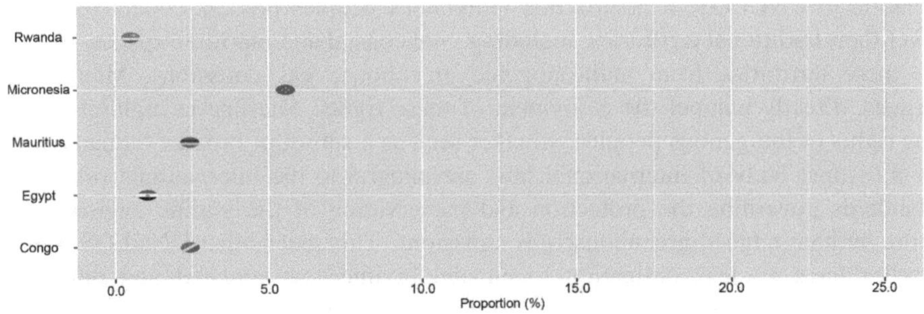

Fig. 5.7 Proportional representation in written statement: Remedies. *Source* Authors

underlying concepts of 'violation', 'breach', and 'unlawful' acts were discussed as triggers for responsibility, alongside arguments concerning 'compliance' and 'non-compliance' with international obligations. Even though the COSIS request for an advisory opinion[122] did not address state responsibility, five states of the Global South—specifically, Micronesia, Egypt, Mauritius, Rwanda and Congo—addressed the subject in their written submissions (Fig. 5.7).

Rwanda[123] contended that the topic of liability for damages arising from internationally wrongful acts was not the object of the request submitted by COSIS, which was limited to seeking clarification on the existing obligations. On the other hand, Micronesia, Mauritius, Egypt and Congo claimed that the obligations under UNCLOS should be interpreted alongside climate change and environmental norms, as well as the ILC's Articles on Responsibility of States for Internationally Wrongful Acts (ARSIWA). This argument aligns with the discussion that state responsibility stemming from climate change should involve the articulation between the general rules of international law and the specific rules on the law of the sea and the UNFCCC regime.[124]

While not explicitly addressing the topic of reparations, Mauritius[125] contended that neglecting climate change would lead to non-compliance with international obligations established under the UNCLOS and constitute a breach of the rules governing the UNFCCC. Egypt[126] reasoned briefly on the theme of reparation for damages as a consequence of the violation of an obligation, alongside cessation. It based these claims by referencing Article 235 of the UNCLOS on state responsibility, which must be interpreted in conjunction with the ARSIWA. Micronesia and Congo further discussed how reparations under this particular context could be implemented. Micronesia[127] referred to 'full reparation' to include restoring the

[122] Commission of Small Island States on Climate Change and International Law, *supra* note 21.

[123] Written Statement of the Republic of Rwanda, *supra* note 162. at para 58.

[124] B. Mayer (2018).

[125] Written Statement of Mauritius, *supra* note 161.at paras 87–88.

[126] Written Statement of the Arab Republic of Egypt, *supra* note 158. at para 90.

[127] Written Statement of the Federated States of Micronesia, *supra* note 176. at para 67.

marine environment to its pre-pollution condition, when possible, as well as compensating the community affected by the pollution. It added that reparations should encompass contributions to the loss and damage fund under the UNFCCC and the Paris Agreement, and/or to liability funds under the International Maritime Organization and the International Seabed Authority. Congo[128] dedicated an entire section to discussing state responsibility under Article 235 of the UNCLOS and the imposition of 'remedial obligations'. By arguing that reparation should include cessation and *restitution in integrum*, Congo claimed that reparation mechanisms must consider the urgency of combating climate change, the scientific data, and the irreparability of the damage affecting the international community.

Furthermore, Micronesia,[129] Mauritius,[130] and Congo[131] elaborated on specific aspects of state responsibility during their oral presentations. Micronesia underscored that rules of State responsibility, including those concerning reparations (such as restitution, compensation, and satisfaction), represent fundamental international legal obligations. It argued that the Tribunal should adopt a holistic view, integrating these "secondary rules" of responsibility—which themselves contain obligations leading to the prevention, reduction, and control of marine pollution—into the current advisory proceeding, asserting that adherence to such rules is essential for addressing marine environmental issues. Congo elaborated on the timing of this responsibility, positing that liability should be engaged not just when irreversible damage has occurred, but also when States fail to take necessary preventative measures to meet climate targets, stressing that the cumulative nature of emissions and causation issues should not allow States to evade their individual responsibility. Mauritius firmly asserted that Article 235 of UNCLOS engages state responsibility for fulfilling obligations to protect the marine environment from climate change, clarifying that a failure to meet these duties, particularly by not adhering to the best available scientific evidence (like IPCC findings), gives rise to liability under international law. Mauritius also highlighted that those States with the highest historical emissions bear the greatest responsibility for current reductions. Together, these statements advocate for a holistic interpretation of state responsibility, urging the Tribunal to affirm clear obligations that compel measures for marine environmental protection and address the consequences of non-compliance.

References

Bastos (2024) Looking at the Case Law of the European Court of Human Rights Through the Lens of the International Law of the Sea. In: Siig K, Feldtmann B, Billing FMW (eds) The United Nations Convention on the Law of the Sea: a System of Regulation, p 115

[128] Written Statement of the Democratic Republic of the Congo, *supra* note 167. at paras 78–84.

[129] Oral Statement of Micronesia, 41–42.

[130] Oral Statement of Mauritius, 30–31.

[131] Oral Statement of the Democratic Republic of the Congo, 25–26.

Billing (2024) Human Rights from Within the UNCLOS System. In: Siig K, Feldtmann B (eds) The United Nations Convention on the Law of the Sea: a System of Regulation, p 106
d'Aspremont (2021) International Law as a Crisis Discourse: the Peril of Wordlessness. In: Mbengue MM, D'Aspremont J (eds) Crisis Narratives in International Law, p 69
Hunter D, Salzman J, Zaelke D (2022) International Environmental Law and Policy, 6th edn
International Tribunal for the Law of the Sea (2015a), Request for Advisory Opinion submitted by the Sub-Regional Fisheries Commission, Advisory Opinion (2 April 2015) ITLOS Reports, p. 21, §54–57
International Tribunal for the Law of the Sea (2015b), Request for Advisory Opinion submitted by the Sub-Regional Fisheries Commission, Advisory Opinion (2 April 2015) ITLOS Reports, p. 21, §59–60
International Tribunal for the Law of the Sea (2015c), Request for Advisory Opinion submitted by the Sub-Regional Fisheries Commission, Advisory Opinion (2 April 2015) ITLOS Reports, p. 5
ITLOS Statute, Article 21: The jurisdiction of the Tribunal comprises all disputes and all applications submitted to it in accordance with this Convention and all matters specifically provided for in any other agreement which confers jurisdiction on the Tribunal
Mayer B (2018) The International Law on Climate Change, 1st edn
Ngang (2017) Differentiated Responsibilities under International Law and the Right to Development Paradigm for Developing Countries. Human Rights & International Legal Discourse 11:265
Otten (2016) Narratives in International Law. KritV, CritQ, RCrit Kritische Vierteljahresschrift Für Gesetzgebung Und Rechtswissenschaft / Critical Quarterly for Legislation and Law/ Revue Critique Trimestrielle de Jurisprudence Et de Législation 99:187 at 196
Sands P et al (2018) Principles of International Environmental Law, 4th edn
Singh (2022) Tracing the "Common but Differentiated Responsibilities" (CBDR) Principle under Climate Change Regime. Indian J Law Justice 13:251
Tanaka (n 3) 530. The only references to advisory opinions under the law of the sea are those of the ITLOS Sea-Bed Disputes Chamber in response to a request from the Assembly or Council of the International Seabed Authority, see UNCLOS, Article 159(10), 191; Annex VI, Art 40(2)
Voigt (2021) International Environmental Responsibility and Liability. SSRN Electron J
Written Statement of Mauritius, Request For An Advisory Opinion Submitted By The Commission Of Small Island States On Climate Change And International Law (2023) International Tribunal for the Law of the Sea. Available at https://www.itlos.org/fileadmin/itlos/documents/cases/31/written_statements/1/C31-WS-1-12-Mauritius.pdf. at para 70
Written Statement of the Arab Republic of Egypt, Request For An Advisory Opinion Submitted By The Commission Of Small Island States On Climate Change And International Law (2023) International Tribunal for the Law of the Sea. Available at https://itlos.org/fileadmin/itlos/documents/cases/31/written_statements/1/C31-WS-1-17-Egypt.pdf. at para 65
Written Statement of the Democratic Republic of the Congo, Request For An Advisory Opinion Submitted By The Commission Of Small Island States On Climate Change And International Law (2023) International Tribunal for the Law of the Sea. Available at https://itlos.org/fileadmin/itlos/documents/cases/31/written_statements/1/C31-WS-1-1-RD_Congo_translation_ITLOS.pdf. at para 215
Written Statement of the Federated States of Micronesia, Request For An Advisory Opinion Submitted By The Commission Of Small Island States On Climate Change And International Law (2023) International Tribunal for the Law of the Sea. Available at https://itlos.org/fileadmin/itlos/documents/cases/31/written_statements/1/C31-WS-1-30-FS_Micronesia_01.pdf. at para 60
Written Statement of the Federative Republic of Brazil, Request For An Advisory Opinion Submitted By The Commission Of Small Island States On Climate Change And

International Law (2023) International Tribunal for the Law of the Sea. Available at https://itlos.org/fileadmin/itlos/documents/cases/31/written_statements/1/C31-WS-1-18-Brazil_01.pdf. at paras 17–19
Written Statement of the People's Republic of Bangladesh, Request For An Advisory Opinion Submitted By The Commission Of Small Island States On Climate Change And International Law, 2023, International Tribunal for the Law of the Sea. Available at https://www.itlos.org/fileadmin/itlos/documents/cases/31/written_statements/1/C31-WS-1-21-Bangladesh.pdf para 2
Written Statement of the People's Republic of China, Request For An Advisory Opinion Submitted By The Commission Of Small Island States On Climate Change And International Law (2023) International Tribunal for the Law of the Sea. Available at https://itlos.org/fileadmin/itlos/documents/cases/31/written_statements/1/C31-WS-1-8-China__transmission_ltr._.pdf. at paras 29 and 36
Written Statement of the Republic of Chile, Request For An Advisory Opinion Submitted By The Commission Of Small Island States On Climate Change And International Law (2023) International Tribunal for the Law of the Sea. Available at https://itlos.org/fileadmin/itlos/documents/cases/31/written_statements/1/C31-WS-1-20-Chile_01.pdf. at para 57–58
Written Statement of the Republic of Djibouti, Request For An Advisory Opinion Submitted By The Commission Of Small Island States On Climate Change And International Law (2023) International Tribunal for the Law of the Sea. Available at https://itlos.org/fileadmin/itlos/documents/cases/31/written_statements/1/C31-WS-1-31-Djibouti_translation_ITLOS.pdf. at para 57
Written Statement of the Republic of Guatemala, Request For An Advisory Opinion Submitted By The Commission Of Small Island States On Climate Change And International Law (2023) International Tribunal for the Law of the Sea. Available at https://www.itlos.org/fileadmin/itlos/documents/cases/31/written_statements/1/C31-WS-1-26-Guatemala_01.pdf paras 8–25
Written Statement of the Republic of India, Request For An Advisory Opinion Submitted By The Commission Of Small Island States On Climate Change And International Law (2023) International Tribunal for the Law of the Sea. Available at https://itlos.org/fileadmin/itlos/documents/cases/31/written_statements/3/C31-WS-3-4-India.pdf. at paras 15–28
Written Statement of the Republic of Mozambique, Request For An Advisory Opinion Submitted By The Commission Of Small Island States On Climate Change And International Law (2023) International Tribunal for the Law of the Sea. Available at https://itlos.org/fileadmin/itlos/documents/cases/31/written_statements/1/C31-WS-1-10-Mozambique_01.pdf. at para 3.48
Written Statement of the Republic of Nauru, Request For An Advisory Opinion Submitted By The Commission Of Small Island States On Climate Change And International Law (2023) International Tribunal for the Law of the Sea. Available at https://itlos.org/fileadmin/itlos/documents/cases/31/written_statements/1/C31-WS-1-22-Nauru.pdf. at para 5
Written Statement of the Republic of Rwanda, Request For An Advisory Opinion Submitted By The Commission Of Small Island States On Climate Change And International Law (2023) International Tribunal for the Law of the Sea. Available at https://itlos.org/fileadmin/itlos/documents/cases/31/written_statements/3/C31-WS-3-1-Rwanda.pdf. at paras 303 and 290–314
Written Statement of the Republic of Sierra Leone, Request For An Advisory Opinion Submitted By The Commission Of Small Island States On Climate Change And International Law (2023) International Tribunal for the Law of the Sea. Available at https://itlos.org/fileadmin/itlos/documents/cases/31/written_statements/1/C31-WS-1-29-Sierra_Leone.pdf. at para 62
Written Statement of the Socialist Republic of Vietnam, Request For An Advisory Opinion Submitted By The Commission Of Small Island States On Climate Change And International Law (2023) International Tribunal for the Law of the Sea. Available at https://itlos.org/fileadmin/itlos/documents/cases/31/written_statements/3/C31-WS-3-3-Viet_Nam.pdf. at para 5.1–5.3

Chapter 6
Articulating States' Narratives in Political and Legal Arenas: Uncovering a South-South Divide

Abstract This chapter explores how Global South states strategically construct narratives in international legal and political arenas to advance distinct climate agendas. It examines the interplay between political discourse at COPs 26, 27 and 28 and legal arguments presented before the ITLOS advisory proceedings on climate change. The chapter identifies two predominant narratives. The first, adopted by emerging economies such as Brazil, India, China, and Egypt, emphasizes developmental priorities and the principles of CBDR-RC, cooperation, and assistance, resisting legal interpretations that could impose greater obligations. The second, advanced by the most vulnerable states—including small island nations and least developed countries—foregrounds human rights, state responsibility, and survival imperatives, calling for urgent action and reparation. These narratives reveal a divide within the Global South and demonstrate how international law is mobilized not only as a normative framework but also as a strategic tool to shape and contest global climate governance. The chapter underscores that legal proceedings before ICTs serve both as platforms for normative clarification and as catalysts for broader political transformation.

Keywords Global South · Climate change litigation · South-South divide

This chapter investigates the intricate interplay of state narratives in political and legal contexts. Portraying international law as a 'struggle between different political interests',[1] the narratives advanced before ICTs must be understood within the broader context of international politics. These narratives may emerge from specific political strategies and serve broader political objectives. The examination of the political context articulated by Global South states at the UNFCCC COPs 26,

[1] A. Orakhelashvili (2022).

P. Wojcikiewicz Almeida et al., *Uncovering Global South Narratives in ITLOS Advisory Proceedings on Climate Change*, SpringerBriefs in Law,
https://doi.org/10.1007/978-3-032-08427-9_6

27, and 28, combined with the categorical content analysis technique of the legal arguments presented before the ITLOS advisory proceedings on climate change[2] contributes to uncovering states' narratives.

The present examination outlines two main patterns of narratives emerging from the Global South states that reinforce a South-South divide,[3] especially when considering the substantial disparities in development and the growing threat of climate-generated vulnerabilities. The first subsection elaborates on a narrative predominantly articulated by developing states that have extensively utilized the legal categories of the *CBDR-RC principle* and the *duties of cooperation and assistance* in their submissions to the Tribunal. This analysis highlights developmental and economic concerns that also surfaced in their statements at the analyzed COPs (6.1). The second subsection focuses on a narrative more prominent among the most economically and socially vulnerable states that have placed greater emphasis on the legal categories of *human rights* and *state responsibility* in their submissions to the Tribunal. This reflects their stance at the COPs, when the same states urged the international community to address the climate urgency as for them it represents a matter of imminent survival (6.2).

6.1 Narratives Uncovering Developmental Interests

The varying experiences of climate urgency influence the strategies adopted by international actors. This differentiation is reflected in the arguments presented before the Tribunal, which often reflect underlying political concerns, such as the potential impact of climate change mitigation measures on development and economic growth. Indeed, emerging countries within the Global South—especially Brazil, India, China and Egypt—presented a legal narrative before the Tribunal underpinning their developmental interests. This pattern was also observed in their political statements at the COPs, where their discourses on climate action often reflected an underlying apprehension about the potential impacts on their economies and development.

Countries emphasizing CBDR-RC and the duties of cooperation and assistance constructed a narrative centered on the interpretation of environmental obligations, as revealed by the categorical analysis, in light of their socioeconomic realities. Brazil, Vietnam, Egypt and India[4] devoted a greater portion of their submissions to advocating for the principle of differentiated responsibilities for states based on their level of development. Brazil, India, and China[5] dedicated considerable space in their statements to address the need for financial and technical support from

[2] Cardoso Sampaio and Lycarião (2021).

[3] Ferreira (2018).

[4] See categorical content analysis on the Principle of Common But Differentiated Responsibilities and Respective Capabilities in Sect. 5.2 of Chap. 5.

[5] See categorical content analysis on the Duties of Cooperation and Assistance in Sect. 5.3 of Chap. 5.

developed countries to meet climate challenges while ensuring their development needs. In emphasizing these legal categories, such states underscored the historical emissions of developed countries as major contributors to the current climate crisis, thereby strengthening the legal foundation for their demand for differentiated responsibilities. When claiming for a fairer allocation of obligations related to climate change, the intention was to ensure that developed countries should bear the largest responsibilities, despite the increased GHG emissions of emerging countries from the Global South.[6]

The political context underlying the narratives advanced before the ITLOS advisory proceedings on climate change reveals direct references by some emerging states, including Egypt (at COPs[7] 27 and 28[8]), China (at COP 28[9]) and Brazil (at COP 28[10]), to the CBDR-RC principle and their increased need for financial assistance and technology transfer from developed nations. These countries focused on the North-South disparities around historical emissions, asserting that 'developed nations' bear the greatest responsibility for funding climate action. These states prioritised sustainable development in their discourses, presenting it as a strategy to reconcile economic growth with ecological responsibility. This political context exposes preferences and interests of the states that can potentially 'affect or shape the content of rights and obligations of states in specific disputes, controversies and conflicts'.[11] This connection undermines the belief of 'autonomous legal foundations of normative law' by revealing the political background that exists behind positive law.[12]

For instance, political interests have shaped the storyline behind the allocation of different obligations regarding nationally determined contributions (NDCs), cooperation and assistance between 'developed and developing countries'.[13] The development of the climate change legal framework has consistently faced debate, with the North-South model of differentiation experiencing political pressure throughout its evolution.[14] Primarily, the UNFCCC established a legal framework based on this dichotomy, in which developed countries were required to implement binding national mitigation policies while developing nations were encouraged to adopt mitigation programs voluntarily with support from developed countries.[15] The Kyoto Protocol reinforced this binary approach by assigning mitigation

[6] Hurrell and Sengupta (2012).

[7] Egypt (2021).

[8] Egypt (2022).

[9] China (2023).

[10] Brazil (2023).

[11] Orakhelashvili (2022).

[12] Burley (1993).

[13] Ferreira (2018).

[14] Ibid.

[15] Art. 3.1 and Art. 4.2 (a), United Nations Framework Convention on Climate Change 1992, 1771 U.N.T.S. 107.

obligations exclusively to Annex I countries—developed countries—during its first commitment period.[16] However, this model faced increasing challenges as emerging economies from the Global South with significant and growing emissions resisted stricter commitments.[17] The Paris Agreement, despite continuing to emphasize the leadership role of developed nations in emissions reductions and financial support,[18] marked a significant shift when asserting that all state parties are required to formulate, communicate, and update their NDCs. Therefore, it stressed the universal responsibility rather than a strict North-South divide.[19] This reverberates the idea that the climate regime is a politically and socially constructed process which has been historically embedded in contradictions, divergent narratives, and power imbalances.[20]

The acceptance or denial of the ITLOS's jurisdictional authority by a state bringing a climate change-related issue before the Tribunal can be seen as an indication of its specific perspective on the role of international law in addressing climate change.[21] Brazil, India and China were the only Global South states to reject the Tribunal's jurisdiction to issue an advisory opinion, whereas Egypt did not address the matter.[22] China[23] also participated in the previous advisory proceedings before the ITLOS, equally denying the advisory jurisdiction of the full Tribunal. While the arguments presented to reject the Tribunal's jurisdictional authority were based on procedural provisions, this positionality may indicate that there are some underlying political interests in preventing the Tribunal from delivering an opinion on the topic. It has been argued that all international disputes are justiciable, even if politically sensitive.[24] However, a more cautious understanding portrayed ICTs as not the most effective venue for resolving disputes that deal with systemic problems or with significant political dimensions, as they often require comprehensive, policy-oriented approaches[25] and that the parties concerned have no control over the outcome, as in opposition to negotiation practices.

Thus, the interplay between law and politics provides valuable insights into the factors that influence the legal positions adopted by states,[26] as evidenced in the narratives of emerging countries from the Global South before the ITLOS

[16] Art. 4.1 and Art. 4.2, Ibid.

[17] Hurrell and Sengupta (2012).

[18] Art. 4.4 and Art. 9.3, Paris Agreement to the United Nations Framework Convention on Climate Change, 2015, T.I.A.S. No. 16–1104.

[19] Ferreira (2018).

[20] F. Sultana (2024).

[21] d'Aspremont (2022).

[22] See categorical content analysis on Jurisdiction in Sect. 5.1 of Chap. 5.

[23] Written Statement of the People's Republic of China, 'Request for an Advisory Opinion submitted by the Sub-Regional Fisheries Commission (SRFC), *International Tribunal for the Law of the Sea* (Written Statement of the People's Republic of China 2015).

[24] H. Lauterpacht (1933).

[25] V Lowe (2012).

[26] Ferreira (2018).

proceedings on climate change. This articulation assisted in uncovering the 'hidden cargo of the script', which represents the underlying dynamics and interests that drive the construction of a narrative.[27] This perceived *narrative uncovering developmental interes*ts disclosed an approach that seeks to leverage the existing legal framework to avoid assuming greater responsibilities that could harm their economic interests. It suggests that emerging economies from the Global South, especially Brazil, China, India and Egypt, although affected by the consequences of climate change, still require room for manoeuvre for their economic development. Their substantive arguments underscore a broader urge for climate action to act as a catalyst for sustainable development rather than an obstacle to growth.

6.2 Narratives Uncovering Vulnerabilities

The most vulnerable states in the Global South unfolded a narrative highlighting the urgency of tackling the severe social impacts of climate change, the recognition of international responsibility and a broader legal interpretation linking climate and oceanic obligations. These arguments were also evident in the political discourses at the COPs, which highlighted the disproportional impact of climate change on developing countries. It shows that understanding the political context surrounding the legal submissions assists in uncovering the states' narratives, each reflecting individual experiences and unique geopolitical knowledge that confronts the idea of a single framing of the issue.[28] This proposition, by foregrounding other perspectives, highlights the power of narratives as counter-hegemonic storytelling and transformative tools in international law.[29] It is precisely through narratives that 'the perspective of the subaltern, of the colonised State, or to colonialised relationships' may grasp international law's attention.[30]

Most of the African and Small Island states specifically outlined their vulnerabilities in their submissions before the ITLOS proceedings on climate change. This reflects the uneven distribution of existential threats posed by the climate emergency, with black individuals and vulnerable communities experiencing its impacts more severely.[31] The categorical content analysis demonstrated that the most vulnerable states in the Global South advanced human rights concerns by reinforcing a direct impact inflicted on the rights of their population. Despite the singularity of distinct narratives shaped by subjective experiences,[32] Nauru, Micronesia, Mauritius, and

[27] Otten (2016).

[28] Sultana (2024).

[29] Delgado (1989).

[30] Otten (2016).

[31] Valayden (2024).

[32] Otten (2016).

Congo[33] were mostly concerned with the human rights implications of climate change and argued for stronger protection under international law. A critical point of contention revolved around the applicable legal framework, on which these countries argued for a connection between human rights, climate change, and the law of the sea, emphasising the interrelated nature of these issues. It posits that environmental protection is intrinsically linked to the enjoyment of human rights, such as the right to life, health, and a healthy environment. This underscores the role of international law as a framework for navigating crises and a valuable discursive tool that can be invoked to respond to such challenges.[34]

The term 'climate apartheid' has been used to underscore the inherent inequality in of the climate urgency, where some possess the economic means to escape its worst impacts while others are disproportionately burdened and suffer the consequences.[35] The concept of 'urgency' contains in itself a vocabulary of timeframe not equally perceived by all actors. Those most severely impacted by the consequences of climate change are the ones who most urgently demand rapid action. Micronesia, Congo, Egypt, and Mauritius[36] were the only countries to address in their submissions the topic of state responsibility, stressing the obligation of states to repair the damage caused by climate change. While not directly within the scope of the advisory opinion, these countries, representing some of the most vulnerable countries, used the opportunity to address the matter. Their narrative prioritized their survival and emphasized the responsibility of the major contributors to the climate crisis.

The connection between the positions adopted by these countries at the COPs and the ITLOS advisory proceedings confirms how international law can provide a 'louder voice' to small states.[37] Similarly, the most vulnerable states have also mobilised international forums to advocate for more equitable and just climate governance. The discourses of Small Island states at the COPs underscore the asymmetries inside the Global South and a stronger vulnerability that affects the less developed countries. For instance, Belize at COPs 26,[38] 27,[39] and 28[40] highlighted its vulnerability to climate change due to geographical and economic characteristics. This framing was also emphasised by Nauru[41] and Mauritius[42] at COP 26 and Micronesia at COPs 27[43] and 28.[44] The less developed countries, including

[33] See categorical content analysis on Human Rights in Sect. 5.5 of Chap. 5.

[34] d'Aspremont (2022).

[35] Long (2024).

[36] See categorical content analysis on Remedies in Sect. 5.6 of Chap. 5.

[37] D. Guilfoyle (2023).

[38] Belize (2021).

[39] Belize (2022).

[40] Belize (2023).

[41] Nauru (2021).

[42] Mauritius (2021).

[43] Micronesia (2022).

[44] Micronesia (2023).

Mozambique (COP 27[45]) and Rwanda (COP 28[46]), highlighted their limited adaptive capacities and the severe consequences they face due to climate inaction and the urgent need for safeguarding their vulnerable communities and ecosystems.

The urgent measures necessary to avert the climate catastrophe require international law to move beyond crisis narratives to avoid wordlessness and preserve its role in guiding global solutions.[47] This challenging task reveals the perspectives of international actors on the role of ICTs in addressing politically sensitive issues. Since litigation is just one phase in a broader political drama, it can be seen as a catalyst to further negotiations by putting parties under pressure and seeking clarification of legal norms.[48]

The extent to which states elaborated on arguments related to the legal category of the *obligation to prevent marine pollution* can be interpreted as an indicator of their trust in the Tribunal's advisory function to catalyze stronger commitments. Countries like Nauru, Bangladesh, Belize, Sierra Leone, Micronesia, Rwanda, Mauritius, and Chile[49] were mostly concerned with the connection between the UNCLOS and climate change obligations and with delineating specific obligations, such as laws and regulations to be adopted, monitoring and environmental assessment, and enforcement of the measures. This reflects a view that international adjudication could potentially help in the negotiation process by clarifying duties and specific criteria—e.g. due diligence standards—which would encourage countries to adopt more ambitious NDCs in the political forums. As adjudication operates in interaction with political institutions, it can offer a mechanism for dialogue that may play a decisive role in shaping international bargaining dynamics as a strategic step within a larger political process.[50]

The articulation between the political context and the categorical content analysis revealed a narrative uncovering the vulnerabilities of the states from the Global South that are more affected by the climate crisis and have not benefited from industrialisation or late development. Their storyline highlighted the particular vulnerabilities of these countries while reclaiming urgent action from developed states. Human rights were a prominent subject both in political discourses and throughout the legal arguments presented. Similarly, the topic of state responsibility was mobilized to demand a cessation of the violation and reparation for the damage caused by climate change. The arguments developed to establish a link between state obligations under UNCLOS and climate-related effects suggest confidence in the Tribunal's ability to render a favourable outcome that clarifies the broader scope of state obligations. It confirms that this *fora* represents an opportunity for smaller and less powerful states to assert their

[45] Mozambique (2022).

[46] Rwanda (2023).

[47] d'Aspremont (2022).

[48] Scott (2014).

[49] Bangladesh (2023), Micronesia (2023), Rwanda (2023), Chile (2023).

[50] Scott (2014).

interests when compared to traditional diplomatic forums.[51] Moreover, beyond resolving a specific dispute, initiating legal action can serve to raise international awareness of the issue, exert political pressure, and garner global support for the cause,[52] which is crucial for the most vulnerable states urging the international community to promptly address the climate issue.

References

Burley (1993) International law and international relations theory: a Dual Agenda. Am J Int Law 87:205 at 245

Cardoso Sampaio R, Lyciarão D (2021), Análise de Conteúdo Categorial: manual de Aplicação

D'Aspremont J (2022) International law as a crisis discourse: the Peril of Wordlessness. In d'Aspremont J, Mbengue MM (eds) Crisis Narratives in International Law, 1ed. Brill, p 70

Delgado (1989) Storytelling for oppositionists and others: a Plea for Narrative. Michigan Law Review 87:2411

Guilfoyle D (2023) Small States, legal statecraft and opening submissions in the ITLOS Climate Change Advisory Proceedings, 18 September 2023, Blog of the European Journal of International Law (EJIL:Talk!)

Ferreira (2018) Differentiation in international environmental law: has Pragmatism Displaced Considerations of Justice? In: Craik N, et al (eds) Global Environmental Change and Innovation in International Law, 1st edn. 21

Hurrell A and Sengupta S (2012) Emerging powers, North-South relations and global climate politics. International Affairs (Royal Institute of International Affairs 1944-) 88: 463, at 467.

Lauterpacht H (1933) The function of law in the international community. Oxford University Press, New York, Oxford: Clarendon Press xxiv, p 469

Long (2024) The coloniality of climate apartheid—Excising colonial legacies in climate development and governance. Confronting Climate Coloniality: Decolonizing Pathways for Climate Justice, 1st edn. 33

Lowe V (2012) The function of litigation in international society. Iclq 61:209

Orakhelashvili A (ed) (2022) Research handbook on the theory and history of international law, Second edition, paperback edition, at 255

Otten (2016) 'Narratives in International Law', 99 KritV, CritQ, RCrit. Kritische Vierteljahresschrift Für Gesetzgebung Und Rechtswissenschaft / Critical Quarterly for Legislation and Law/Revue Critique Trimestrielle de Jurisprudence et de Législation 187, at 197–209

Scott (2014) Litigation versus dispute resolution through political processes. In: Klein N Litigating international law disputes, 1st edn. 24

Sultana F (2024) Confronting climate coloniality: decolonizing Pathways for Climate Justice, 1st edn. 50

Valayden (2024) The politics of "Heaviness" in climate emergency. In: Confronting climate coloniality: decolonizing pathways for climate justice, 1st edn. 33, at 81

Written Statement of the People's Republic of China (2015) Request for an Advisory Opinion submitted by the Sub-Regional Fisheries Commission (SRFC), International Tribunal for the Law of the Sea

[51] Guilfoyle (2023).

[52] Scott (2014).

Chapter 7
Conclusion

Abstract This chapter explores how Global South states use international legal proceedings—specifically the advisory proceedings before the International Tribunal for the Law of the Sea (ITLOS) on climate change—as platforms to articulate their foreign legal policy. Drawing from the concept that international law is intertwined with political interests, the study examines the written and oral submissions of Global South states alongside their high-level statements at the UNFCCC COPs. Through categorical analysis, the research identifies two dominant narratives among the Global South: one centred on developmental interests, as seen in the submissions by Brazil, China, India, and Vietnam; and another focused on vulnerabilities, advanced by small island states and African nations. These differences point to a South–South divide in climate legal-political positioning, despite shared historical legacies. The chapter further demonstrates how participation in advisory proceedings, even when jurisdiction is contested, serves as a strategic tool for states to project their international agendas. By positioning legal narratives within a broader political context, this study shows that international courts and tribunals (ICTs) are not neutral spaces, but contested arenas where law and foreign policy intersect.

Keywords Foreign legal policy · International Tribunal for the Law of the Sea (ITLOS) · Narratives · South–South divide

The term 'foreign legal policy'[1] refers to the idea that international law is not an abstract or metaphysical construct but is deeply intertwined with the actions of states in pursuit of their national interests, which influence the formation of international

[1] Lacharrière (2023).

P. Wojcikiewicz Almeida et al., *Uncovering Global South Narratives in ITLOS Advisory Proceedings on Climate Change*, SpringerBriefs in Law,
https://doi.org/10.1007/978-3-032-08427-9_7

norms and rules.[2] Considering this concept, the new wave of requests for advisory opinions and the increased participation of states in these proceedings could be seen as essential to the future of international law and climate governance. This book exposed that states' national interests and political stances were articulated with their legal arguments submitted to the ITLOS advisory proceedings on climate change. Those arguments were understood as narratives since jurists often describe the meaning of the law through a narration process.[3] By uncovering the storylines embedded in the Global South countries' submissions to the ITLOS and articulating them with their high-level statements at the COPs, the study demonstrated that the narratives presented before ICTs can be seen as part of a broader political context in which states utilize different international arenas to advance their interests. This underscores that the quest undertaken by different countries to achieve their foreign policy objectives plays an important role in shaping international law.

The joint analysis of the written submissions with the high-level statements at the COPs suggests not only the connection between states' narratives at ICTs and their broader political stances but also the existence of different storylines among the Global South countries. Hence, despite their loosely shared history of colonialism, external influence and inequalities, the distinct narratives advanced before ITLOS echo different interests among them. This confirms that, although the history of the Global South and the roots of climate change intersect as products of colonisation and capitalist expansion,[4] the accelerating pace of climate change is fostering South-South differences that transcend traditional political divisions.[5]

The combination of political context and legal arguments discussed in section 3 uncovered two major narratives, revealing a South-South divide. These narratives refer, on the one hand, to the protection of *developmental interests*, and to the assertion of *vulnerabilities*, on the other. The findings indicate that states such as Brazil, Vietnam, India, and China framed their narratives before the ITLOS around *developmental interests*, advocating for differentiated responsibilities and emphasizing the need for financial support from the Global North to fight against climate change impacts. At the COPs, these states similarly stressed the importance of balancing economic growth, poverty-fighting and environmental care with greater emphasis than other countries from the Global South. In contrast, narratives centred on *vulnerability* highlighted human rights as a key argument in the written statements submitted by countries such as Nauru, Micronesia, Mauritius, and Congo. This was frequently articulated with the call for accountability and reparative measures, a stance supported by Micronesia, Congo, Egypt, Mauritius, and Rwanda. Furthermore, countries including Bangladesh, Belize, Sierra Leone, Micronesia, Rwanda, Mauritius, and Chile linked state obligations under UNCLOS to climate impacts. At the COPs, these nations reinforced their calls for urgent mitigation

[2] Mégret (2021).

[3] Devinat (2016).

[4] Murcott and Tigre (2024) 1.; and Long (2024).

[5] Sultana (2024), and Whyte (2017).

support from developed countries and highlighted their stronger exposition of climate change impacts based on economic and geographical conditions.

In addition, it is worth noting that some of the countries advancing a narrative centred on *developmental interests*, namely Brazil, India and China, did not recognize the jurisdiction of the Tribunal to issue the advisory opinion as requested by COSIS,[6] whereas Egypt did not address the matter. China[7] also participated in the previous advisory proceedings before the ITLOS, equally denying the advisory jurisdiction of the full Tribunal. While the arguments were based on procedural provisions, they may indicate political interests in preventing the Tribunal from delivering an opinion on the topic. On the other hand, African countries (except Egypt) and small island states, having focused their narrative on *vulnerabilities*, consented to the jurisdiction of ITLOS.

If all international disputes are justiciable even if politically sensitive,[8] the position adopted by some economic and politically powerful Global South states may demonstrate a more cautious understanding of the role of ICTs as not the most effective venue for resolving disputes dealing with systemic problems or with significant political dimensions, as they often require comprehensive, policy-oriented approaches.[9] In contrast, the position adopted by African countries and small island states might indicate that the most vulnerable countries tend to rely on ICTs to advance their interests. These findings also confirm how international legal *fora* can give more visibility to the demands and necessities of nations with little material power.[10] This reality reinforces the South-South divide as far as substantial arguments are concerned.

Since international law and international politics share the same theoretical space,[11] the narratives advanced by states before ICTs should be seen as part of a broader political background. By framing Global South states' written submissions before the ITLOS within the political context brought by their speeches at the COPs, the book provides strong evidence that the narratives advanced at the advisory proceedings on climate change are deeply connected to states' strategies and interests on foreign policy. In addition, the research demonstrated that the ITLOS was considered a legitimate forum through which most Global South states could advance their objectives. Even though states such as Brazil, India and China did not recognize the jurisdiction of the Tribunal to issue the advisory opinion, they

---

[6] Written Statement of Brazil (2023) paras 5–11; Written Statement of India (2023) paras 5–8; Written Statement of China (2023) paras 6–25. As these countries have rarely appeared before ICTs, their stance in denying ITLOS jurisdiction may not carry substantial weight, as it does not represent an isolated political position with regards to climate change.

[7] Written Statement of the People's Republic of China, 'Request for an Advisory Opinion submitted by the Sub-Regional Fisheries Commission (SRFC), *International Tribunal for the Law of the Sea* (2015).

[8] H. Lauterpacht (1933).

[9] V Lowe (2012).

[10] Guilfoyle (2023).

[11] Burley (1993).

expressed their positions on climate change in their written submissions, indirectly recognizing ICTs as an important arena where politics is also at stake.

Future research could expand on these insights by conducting semi-structured interviews with policymakers, jurists and other state representatives to better articulate foreign policy interests with states' participation before ICTs and related strategies. In order to refine the analysis of narratives as a means to uncover how a story is told, the understanding of the intention behind the narrator's choice of words and the nuances subjacent to the writing style appear to be a subtle but inevitable way forward.

References

Burley (1993) International law and international relations theory: a Dual Agenda. Am J Int Law 87:205, at 245

De Lacharrière G (2023) La Politique Juridique Extérieure. Bruylant

Devinat (2016) Réflexion Sur La Narration Judiciaire Dans Les Jugements De La Cour Suprême Du Canada. Cahiers de Méthodologie Juridique n°30

Guilfoyle D (2023) Small states, legal statecraft and opening submissions in the ITLOS climate change advisory proceedings

Lauterpacht H (1933) The function of law in the international community. Oxford University Press, New York. Oxford: Clarendon Press, pp xxiv, 469

Long (2024) The coloniality of climate apartheid—excising colonial legacies in climate development and governance. Confronting climate coloniality: decolonizing Pathways for Climate Justice 33

Lowe V (2012) The function of litigation in international society. ICLQ 61:209

Mégret F (2021) Foreign legal policy as the background to foreign relations law?: Revisiting Guy de Lacharrière's La politique juridique extérieure. In: Aust HP, Kleinlein T (eds), Encounters between Foreign Relations Law and International Law: Bridges and Boundaries. Cambridge: Cambridge University Press, pp. 108–129

Murcott T (2024) Developments, opportunities, and complexities in global south climate litigation: introduction to the special collection. J Hum Rights Pract 16:1

Sultana F (ed) (2024) Confronting climate coloniality: decolonizing pathways for climate justice, 1st edn. p 50

Whyte (2017) Indigenous climate change studies: indigenizing futures, decolonizing the anthropocene. English Language Notes 153

Written Statement of the Federative Republic of Brazil, Request for an Advisory Opinion Submitted by the Commission of Small Island States on Climate Change and International Law (2023) International Tribunal for the Law of the Sea, available at https://itlos.org/fileadmin/itlos/documents/cases/31/written_statements/1/c31-ws-1-18-brazil_01.pdf. at paras 5–11

Written Statement of the People's Republic of China (2015) Request for an Advisory Opinion submitted by the Sub-Regional Fisheries Commission (SRFC). International Tribunal for the Law of the Sea

Written Statement of the People's Republic of China (2023) Request for an Advisory Opinion Submitted by the Commission of Small Island States on Climate Change and International Law. International Tribunal for the Law of the Sea, available at https://itlos.org/fileadmin/itlos/documents/cases/31/written_statements/1/C31-WS-1-8-China__transmission_ltr._.pdf. at paras 6–25

Written Statement of the Republic of India (2023) Request for an Advisory Opinion Submitted by the Commission of Small Island States on Climate Change and International Law. International Tribunal for the Law of the Sea, available at https://itlos.org/fileadmin/itlos/documents/cases/31/written_statements/3/C31-WS-3-4-India.pdf. at paras 5–8

MIX
Papier aus verantwortungsvollen Quellen
Paper from responsible sources
FSC® C105338

If you have any concerns about our products,
you can contact us on
ProductSafety@springernature.com

In case Publisher is established outside the EU,
the EU authorized representative is:
Springer Nature Customer Service Center GmbH
Europaplatz 3, 69115 Heidelberg, Germany

Printed by Libri Plureos GmbH
in Hamburg, Germany